Complete N(

MERVYN PEAKE was one of the best
tieth century, and author of the celebrated ...
(1946), *Gormenghast* (1950) and *Titus Alone* (1959). Born in China in 1911, he was educated at Tientsin Grammar School, Eltham College in Kent and the Royal Academy Schools. From 1935 he taught life drawing at the Westminster School of Art. After being called up in 1940 he underwent military training, but was invalided out of the army following a breakdown in 1942. He worked for a while as an official War Artist, then in 1945 travelled through Germany recording the after-effects of the war, making drawings of Nazi war criminals, POWs and the concentration camp at Bergen-Belsen. In 1946 he went with his family to live on the island of Sark, returning in 1949 to teach life drawing again, this time at the Central School of Art. He was awarded the Heinemann Prize by the Royal Society of Literature in 1951 for his novel *Gormenghast* and poetry collection *The Glassblowers*. His play *The Wit to Woo* was performed at the Arts Theatre in 1957 but did not prove a critical success, and he suffered a second breakdown after its failure. He was diagnosed with Parkinson's disease in 1958, and died ten years later.

R.W. MASLEN is Senior Lecturer at the University of Glasgow. His publications include editions of Mervyn Peake's *Collected Poems* (Carcanet, 2008) and Sir Philip Sidney's *Apology for Poetry* (2002), as well as books on Elizabethan prose fiction and Shakespeare's comedies. He has also written a number of essays on Renaissance literature and twentieth-century fantasy.

G. PETER WINNINGTON is the author of an acclaimed biography of Peake, *Mervyn Peake's Vast Alchemies*, and of *The Voice of the Heart: The Working of Mervyn Peake's Imagination*, a major critical study of Peake's oeuvre. The leading Peake scholar, he has also edited much of Peake's previously unpublished writing, printing it in the periodical *Peake Studies* (www.peakestudies.com), which he edits.

Fyfield*Books* aim to make available some of the great classics of British and European literature in clear, affordable formats, and to restore often neglected writers to their place in literary tradition.

Fyfield*Books* take their name from the Fyfield elm in Matthew Arnold's 'Scholar Gypsy' and 'Thyrsis'. The tree stood not far from the village where the series was originally devised in 1971.

> *Roam on! The light we sought is shining still.*
> *Dost thou ask proof? Our tree yet crowns the hill,*
> *Our Scholar travels yet the loved hill-side*
>
> from 'Thyrsis'

MERVYN PEAKE

Complete Nonsense

Edited with an introduction by
R.W. MASLEN
and
G. PETER WINNINGTON

Fyfield*Books*
CARCANET

First published in Great Britain in 2011 by
Carcanet Press Limited
Alliance House
Cross Street
Manchester M2 7AQ

Selection and editorial matter copyright © R.W. Maslen
and G. Peter Winnington 2011
Poems and drawings by Mervyn Peake copyright © the Estate of Mervyn Peake

The right of R.W. Maslen and G. Peter Winnington to be identified as
the editors of this work has been asserted by them in accordance
with the Copyright, Designs and Patents Act of 1988
All rights reserved

A CIP catalogue record for this book is available from the British Library

ISBN 978 1 84777 087 5

The publisher acknowledges financial assistance from Arts Council England

Supported by
ARTS COUNCIL
ENGLAND

Typeset by XL Publishing Services, Tiverton
Printed and bound in England by SRP Ltd, Exeter

Contents

Acknowledgements   xiii
Introduction by R.W. Maslen   1
A Note on the Text   14
References and Further Reading   16

COMPLETE NONSENSE

I Saw a Puffin	21
The Song of Lien Tsung	22
Railway Ditties	
Waddon	23
Thornton Heath	23
Norbury	23
Streatham and Balham	23
Green Park	24
You Can Never Be Sure of Your Birron	24
Beard of My Chin	26
You Before Me	26
Although I Love Him	26
Practically Poetry	29
Ode to a Bowler	30
Raft Song of the Conger Eel	31
The Dwarf of Battersea	35
Thank God for a Tadpole	42
About My Ebb and Flow-ziness	42
A Fair Amount of Doziness	43
Ancient Root O Ancient Root	44
The Frivolous Cake	44
Simple, Seldom and Sad	47
Linger Now with Me, Thou Beauty	48
I Married Her in Green	50
Swelter's Song	53
I Cannot Simply Stand and Watch	58
Upon the Summit of a Hill	59

Come, Sit Beside Me Dear, He Said	60
Deliria	63
The Sunlight Lies Upon the Fields	64
Mine Was the One	65
The Threads of Thought Are Not for Me	68
Come Husband! Come, and Ply the Trade	69
How Good It Is to Be Alone (1)	71
How Good It Is to Be Alone (2)	73
Upon My Golden Backbone	76
All Over the Lilac Brine!	78
The Sunlight Falls Upon the Grass	80
The Crocodile	82
The Giraffe	84
My Uncle Paul of Pimlico	86
It Makes a Change	88
What a Day It's Been!	90
How Mournful to Imagine	92
The Jailor and the Jaguar	94
The Camel	96
I Wish I Could Remember	98
I Waxes and I Wanes, Sir	100
The Hippopotamus	102
A Languorous Life	104
Sensitive, Seldom and Sad	106
Roll Them Down	108
One Day When They Had Settled Down	110
Again! Again! and Yet Again	112
Uncle George	113
The King of Ranga-Tanga-Roon	114
I Cannot Give You Reasons	115
The Ballad of Sweet Pighead	116
Hold Fast	120
I Must Begin to Comprehend	122
The Threads Remain	123
White Mules at Prayer	124
O Love, O Death, O Ecstasy	127
Tintinnabulum	128
Squat Ursula	138
The Hideous Root	140
The Men in Bowler Hats Are Sweet	148
Aunts and Uncles	150
The Osseous 'Orse	154

Song of the Castle Poet	156
How White and Scarlet Is that Face	157
O Here It Is and There It Is…	158
Little Spider	161
'It Worries Me to Know'	161
A-Lolling on the Shores of Old Hawaii	166
O'er Seas that Have No Beaches	167
The Bullfrog and the Flies	169
The Rhino and the Lark	170
Richly in the Unctuous Dell	174
Manifold Basket's Song	174
With a One, Two, Up!	176
In Ancient Days	176
O Keep Away	178
O Darling When a Story's Done	179
Undertaker's Song (1)	181
Undertaker's Song (2)	182
Nannie Slagg's Song	183
Fuchsia's Song	183
Nannie Slagg's Lullaby	184
Where the Little Dunderhead	184
Lean Sideways on the Wind	186
Of Pygmies, Palms and Pirates	186
An Angry Cactus Does No Good	188
I Cannot Give the Reasons	189
O Little Fly	191
How Fly the Birds of Heaven	191
Leave the Stronger	193
Fish or Fowl	194
'Shrink! Shrink!'	195
An Old and Crumbling Parapet	196
It Is Most Best	198
The Hours of Night Are Drawing On	198
Over the Pig-Shaped Clouds They Flew	200
Come, Break the News to Me, Sweet Horse!	200
What Though My Jaw	202
The Trouble with Geraniums	202
Crocodiles	203
Along the Cold, Regurgitating Shore	204
I Have My Price	204
Jehovah, Jehovah	205
Synopsis: Over the Border or The Adventures of Footfruit	208

The Adventures of Footfruit or The Enthusiast	211
Another Draft of Footfruit: Chapter 1	217
Crown Me with Hairpins	220
Notes	221
Key to the Figures of Speech	234
Index of Titles	235
Index of First Lines	239

Illustrations

The Figures of Speech were published as a guessing game in a book with this title in 1954. So that the game can still be played, the titles are not given here but on p. 234.

Uncle Jake as a Snake, from *Writings and Drawings* (1974), p. 36   19
Figure of Speech   20
Bird with big bill in boots (not previously published)   21
Chinaman with fish, from *Mervyn Peake Review*, no. 11
   (Autumn 1980), p. 2   22
Figure of Speech   25
'I saw a peacock', from *Ride a Cock-horse* (1940)   27
Figure of Speech   28
'He must be an artist', from *Satire* (December 1934), p. 17*   29
'Ode to a bowler hat', from *Satire* (December 1934), p. 17*   30
Figure of Speech   32
Figure of Speech   33
Rumpelstiltskin, from *Radio Times*, vol. 101, no. 1314
   (17 December 1948), p. 20   34
Manuscript page of the first five stanzas of 'The Dwarf of
   Battersea', from *A Book of Nonsense* (1972), p. 16   36
Old man resting, from *A Book of Nonsense* (1972), p. 88   41
The daily help, from *Facet*, vol. 1, no. 1 (1946), p. 9   43
Figure of Speech   46
Figure of Speech   51
Figure of Speech   52
Flay and Steerpike watch Swelter, from *Peake Studies*, vol. 7,
   no. 2 (April 2001), p. 7   56
Swelter with kitchen urchin from *Titus Groan* (1968),
   facing p. 368   55
Figure of Speech   57
Yak on a hilltop, from *A Book of Nonsense* (1972), p. 38   59
Figure of Speech   62
Figure of Speech   66

Figure of Speech	67
Clown on a smoking horse, from *Mervyn Peake: The Man and his Art* (2006), p. 5	68
Figure of Speech	70
Flat face, from *A Book of Nonsense* (1972), p. 72	72
Figure of Speech	74
Rhymes without Reason (1944), dust wrapper	75
Upon My Golden Backbone	77
All Over the Lilac Brine!	79
The Sunlight Falls upon the Grass	81
The Crocodile	83
The Giraffe	85
My Uncle Paul of Pimlico	87
It Makes a Change	89
What a Day It's Been!	91
How Mournful to Imagine	93
The Jailor and the Jaguar	95
The Camel	97
I Wish I Could Remember	99
I Waxes and I Wanes, Sir	101
The Hippopotamus	103
A Languorous Life	105
Sensitive, Seldom and Sad	107
Stylized horse (not previously published)	109
One Day When They Had Settled Down, from *Peake Studies*, vol. 5, no. 4 (April 1998), back cover*	111
Again! Again! and Yet Again, from *Peake Studies*, vol. 5, no. 4 (April 1998), p. 22*	112
Uncle George, from *Peake Studies*, vol. 5, no. 4 (April 1998), p. 23*	113
The King of Ranga-Tanga-Roon, from *Peake Studies*, vol. 5, no. 4 (April 1998), p. 25*	114
I Cannot Give You Reasons, from *Peake Studies*, vol. 5, no. 4 (April 1998), p. 26*	115
Figure of Speech	118
A Gormenghast professor, from *Mervyn Peake: The Man and his Art* (2006), p. 84	121
Rottcodd in his hammock, from *Peake Studies*, vol. 7, no. 1 (November 2000), pp. 18–19	124
Royal couple, from *A Book of Nonsense* (1974), p. 44	127
Figure of Speech	129

Horned figure with familiar, from *A Book of Nonsense* (1974), p. 50	137
Squat Ursula, from *A Book of Nonsense* (1974), p. 75*	139
Men in conical hats, from *A Book of Nonsense* (1974), p. 64	145
Figure of Speech	149
Aunty Vi, from *A Book of Nonsense* (1974), p. 68*	150
Aunty Flo, from *A Book of Nonsense* (1974), p. 67*	151
Aunty Mig, from *A Book of Nonsense* (1974), p. 69*	152
Uncle Jake, from *A Book of Nonsense* (1974), p. 71*	152
Aunty Jill, from *A Book of Nonsense* (1974), p. 70*	153
Figure of Speech	155
A professor from the MS of *Gormenghast*, from *Mervyn Peake Review*, no. 2 (Spring 1976), p. 19	157
O Here It Is and There It Is…, from *A Book of Nonsense* (1974), p. 46*	159
Have a pear, from *Peake Studies*, vol. 4, no. 1 (Autumn 1994), p. 5	160
Figure of Speech	163
Thorpe and Tintagieu, from *Mr Pye* (1953), p. 68	166
King and dog on beach, from *A Book of Nonsense* (1974), p. 32	167
Figure of Speech	168
Figure of Speech	171
Rhinoceros, London Zoo, from *The Drawings of Mervyn Peake* (1974), p. 41	172
Manifold Basket, B.F., from *Peake Studies*, vol. 2, no. 3 (Winter 1991), p. 47	175
Doctor Willy, from *Peake's Progress* (1978), p. 292	177
Sally Devius, from *Peake's Progress* (1978), p. 290	178
Four Undertakers, from *Peake's Progress* (1978), p. 271	180
Two Undertakers, from *Peake's Progress* (1978), p. 305	182
Figure of Speech	185
Girls, dog and galleon, from *Peake Studies*, vol. 4, no. 1 (Winter 1994), back cover	187
Big nose, big feet, from *A Book of Nonsense* (1974), p. 36	188
Figure of Speech	190
Figure of Speech	192
Man and snake, from *A Book of Nonsense* (1974), p. 28	193
Bird on bird (not previously published)	194
Figure of Speech	197
Figure of Speech	199
Sweet horse, from *A Book of Nonsense* (1974), p. 34*	201
Stout figure with stick, from *A Book of Nonsense* (1974), p. 40	202

Crocodiles, from *A Book of Nonsense* (1974), p. 42*	203
Manimal, from *Peake Studies*, vol. 12, no. 2 (April 2011), p. 4	205
Figure of Speech	206
Figure of Speech	206
Dog-man (1), from *Mervyn Peake: A Personal Memoir* (1984), p. 120	208
Footfruit and dog under the sun, from *A Book of Nonsense* (1974), p. 82*	211
Manuscript page from *New Worlds*, no. 187 (February 1969), p. 43	212
Watching Footfruit, from *A Book of Nonsense* (1974), p. 83*	213
Footfruit climbing hill, from *A Book of Nonsense* (1974), p. 83*	213
Footfruit's boots spout water, from *A Book of Nonsense* (1974), p. 84*	214
Footfruit with his ears like wormcasts, from *A Book of Nonsense* (1974), p. 85*	215
Jackpot laughs like a drain, from *A Book of Nonsense* (1974), p. 85*	215
Dog-Man (2) (not previously published)	217
Jackpot laughs at Footfruit, from *New Worlds*, no. 187 (February 1969), p. 42*	217
Jackpot, from *New Worlds*, no. 187 (February 1969), p. 43*	218
Figure of Speech	219
Noah and cock (not previously published) from the MS of Peake's play *Noah's Ark*	220

* Apart from the *Rhymes without Reason* series (pp. 76–106), only the asterisked drawings were specifically made to accompany nonsense poems. All the others have been chosen by various editors over the years.

Acknowledgements

For help in preparing this book, the editors would like to thank the following: Sebastian Peake, for making the project possible, for giving encouragement at each stage of its development, and for paying Rob Maslen's travel costs for his first trip to Sotheby's; Clare and Fabian Peake for answering queries; Alison Eldred, for finding and scanning dozens of images – so many, indeed, that we haven't been able to use them all; Professor Michael Schmidt, OBE, whose enthusiasm has meant that all Peake's poems will be in print by the end of his centenary year; Judith Willson of Carcanet, the friendliest and most efficient editor imaginable; Peter Selley, Senior Director at Sotheby's, for allowing us to consult the Peake archive at Sotheby's office in Bond Street, and Philip Errington, the Masefield expert and Deputy Director at Sotheby's, for his interest and advice; Rachel Foss and Zoë Wilcox, respectively Curator and Cataloguer of Modern Literary Manuscripts at the British Library, for providing information on the new Peake archive; Pete Bellotte, for sending us transcriptions of interviews he recorded in the 1980s; Jim Boyd, for giving us access to the 'Railway Ditties' inscribed by Peake in his copy of *Titus Groan*, and Madeleine Boyd for scanning them for us; the University of Glasgow, for granting Rob Maslen the research leave during part of which he worked on his share of this edition; Kirsty, Bethany and Grace Maslen, for putting up with all his nonsense as he did so.

R.W. Maslen
G. Peter Winnington
2011

Introduction

Mervyn Peake is one of the great nonsense poets of the twentieth century. His 'rhymes without reason', as he called them, draw inspiration from the great Victorian nonsense poets Lewis Carroll and Edward Lear, but are distinguished by the unique imagination of the man who invented Gormenghast castle, and whose illustrations of Carroll's *Alice* books transformed the inhabitants of Wonderland into honorary subjects of the ancient House of Groan. This volume collects all Peake's nonsense verse for the very first time, and so makes it possible to measure his contribution to the field against the achievements of his two most celebrated predecessors. A rapid glance through its pages will show that he stands up to this daunting comparison remarkably well. And it will show, too, that there is much more of his nonsense verse than anyone could have anticipated.

As well as gathering all Peake's published writings in this mode or genre, we found a great deal of material in the newly assembled Peake archive acquired by the British Library in the spring of 2010. Besides the two notebooks of 'serious' poetry mentioned in the introduction to Peake's *Collected Poems*, dating from c. 1939 and c. 1946 respectively, we found two more exercise books with the titles 'Nonsense Verse' and 'Nonsense / Songs of Nonsense' inscribed on their covers. Both were formerly held in the Bodleian Library, Oxford, under the shelf marks Bod. Dep. Peake 5 and Bod. Dep. Peake 4, and both are stuffed with a treasure trove of bizarre ballads, lunatic lyrics and ridiculous rhymes. The first of these books – identified as 'Nonsense 1' in the notes to this edition – contains drafts of Peake's celebrated ballad *The Rhyme of the Flying Bomb*, which according to Maeve Gilmore he completed 'almost in one burst of writing, day and night' on the island of Sark in about 1947 (*A World Away*, p. 141). This sanctions our tentatively dating Nonsense 1 to that year. The second book (Nonsense 2 in our notes) was evidently being used by Peake towards the end of his working life. The shaky hand in which it is written betrays the onset of the progressive disease that finally killed him, and some drawings and illegible scraps of verse in the later pages bear the subscription 'The Priory 1965 and 1966', dating them to the years when Peake was accommodated in a psychiatric hospital at Roehampton in south London. But the poems in the earlier pages of the book are beautifully transcribed, despite the shakiness of the writer's fingers, and the title 'Songs of Nonsense' suggests that he intended them to form a collection. We have dated this notebook to 1957 and after, 1957 being the year when Peake's physical and psychological condition began to deteriorate rapidly following the failure of his play *The Wit to Woo* on the London stage. Besides these, there are the remains of a third, undatable, exercise book inscribed 'Nonsence Poems', which we refer to by its Bodleian shelf mark (Bod. Dep. Peake 16), and dozens of other verses, both handwritten and typed. Further investigation of the archive may well reveal additional nonsense among the jumbled heaps of paper of which it was partly composed when we consulted it – to say nothing of the material that might emerge from Peake's correspondence in private hands.

The title, then, of this book – *Complete Nonsense* – is not quite accurate. The claim that we are presenting our readers with *all* Peake's nonsense does not stand up to scrutiny, not just because there may be more that we've missed, but also because (as his admirers often point out) everything he wrote was coloured by nonsense: novels, plays, short stories, 'serious' poems, etc. We might more accurately have called our edition *Collected Nonsense Verse*, had it not contained 'The Adventures of Footfruit', which is written in musical prose. The title, then, is complete nonsense, as was the title of another recent edition of Peake's verse, *Collected Poems*. That phrase implied that the collection contained all his poetry between its handsome covers – yet here is a second volume, three years later, with over a hundred poems in it, some of them substantial, about thirty of which have never been published before (though some of these are drafts of poems that *have* been published, so that claim too is a little shaky). The primary reason for leaving out the nonsense from the *Collected Poems* was lack of space; but a secondary reason was that Peake seems to have thought of his nonsense verse as of a wholly different species from his serious poetry – though the categories overlapped, as is evident from the presence of drafts of *The Rhyme of the Flying Bomb* in a notebook devoted to nonsense. In the 1940s he published his book of nonsense rhymes and images, *Rhymes Without Reason*

(1944), separately from his book of poetry, *Shapes and Sounds* (1941), and it looks as though he was planning a second volume of nonsense songs to complement his second poetry collection, *The Glassblowers* (1950), at the point when illness claimed him. We feel, then, that he would have been pleased to see his life's work in these two distinct poetic modes represented in separate volumes, published to coincide with the fortieth anniversary of his death (2008) and the centenary of his birth (2011) respectively.

The present book spans even more of Peake's writing career than the *Collected Poems* does, tracing a golden thread of inspired irrationality that runs through all the literary and artistic metamorphoses of this most protean of creators. Like the *Collected Poems*, it is arranged in chronological order, and we have found it possible to date nearly all the verse with some precision; only one poem remains wholly undated. The first entry in the book was written when he was seven, and it is followed by a cluster of poems from his days as an art student – notably the group we have called the 'Railway Ditties' (pp. 23–4), which were inspired by the names of the stations on the railway line between his home at Wallington, Surrey and the Royal Academy Schools in central London. The last substantial piece – 'The Adventures of Footfruit' (pp. 208-18) – shows him planning an ambitious new departure, a kind of epic prose poem, even as terminal illness was taking hold. In between, as with the serious poems, one gets the sense that there were periods of his life when he composed nonsense with greater or lesser intensity: the years following his release from the army, for instance, culminating in the publication of *Rhymes Without Reason* (1944); or 1947, when he wrote *The Rhyme of the Flying Bomb* on Sark, and produced (as this edition makes clear) a host of other long poems in ballad form to keep it company; the early stages of his final illness, when some of his finest nonsense saw the light of day. As with his serious poetry, his output of nonsense verse slowed down in the early to mid 1950s, when he concentrated on writing plays for stage and radio, but his plays are always breaking into song. Indeed, one of them (*Noah's Ark*) is effectively a musical, while he had plans to turn *The Wit to Woo* into a musical and *Gormenghast* into an opera, and the songs he wrote for them are invariably nonsense, so we have included them in this book. Absurdity was bred into Peake's bones, rooted in his flesh, locked in the fibres of his brain, and he raised it at times to a pitch of seriousness that only Lear and Carroll could match, so that (as he puts it in 'I Cannot Give the Reasons', p. 189) 'it has a beauty / Most proud and terrible / Denied to those whose duty / Is to be cerebral'.

What then is this nonsense, to which Peake devoted so much time and effort in his short but prolific career? Peake himself refused to define it when in 1954 he gave a talk on the BBC about his illustrations for Carroll's *Alice* books. 'In *Alice*,' he explains – despite all the potential terrors the books contain, from the monster Jabberwocky to the bloody-minded Queen of Hearts –

> there is no horror. There is only a certain kind of madness, or nonsense – a very different thing. Madness can be lovely when it's the madness of the imagination and not the madness of pathology. Nonsense can be gentle or riotous. It can clank like a stone in the empty bucket of fatuity. It can take you by the hand and lead you nowhere. It's magic – for to explain it, were that possible, would be to kill it. It swims, plunges, cavorts, and rises in its own element. It's a fabulous fowl. For *non-sense* is not the opposite of good sense. That would be 'Bad Sense'. It's something quite apart – and isn't the opposite of anything. It's something far more rare. Hundreds of books are published year after year. Good sense in many of them: bad sense in many more – but *non-sense*, oh no, that's rarity, a revelation and an art worth all the rest. Perhaps one book in every fifty years glitters with the divine lunacy we call nonsense. ('Alice and Tenniel and Me', p. 22)

Despite Peake's reluctance to 'explain' Carroll's 'certain kind of madness', he says a number of important things about it in this passage. It possesses its own nature, like a newly discovered species, and inhabits its own element – a country of its own, perhaps, with its own rules, or (from the verbs he chooses to describe it: 'swims', 'plunges', 'rises') a medium like water in which there is no bar to movement in any direction. It's not the opposite of 'good sense' because there is often sense or reason in it which, when applied in the context of the element that nonsense inhabits, produces wholly unexpected results. Can we describe nonsense, then, as an arrangement of words on the page without regard to meaning but with careful regard to grammar, form, sound and rhythm? That's more or less right, except that in this mode of writing form gives rise to meaning. Words chosen for their sound and rhythm (or for the startling images or actions they conjure up) acquire a vigorous life of their own, determining the direction of a narrative in verse or prose – leading writer and reader by the hand, to adopt Peake's metaphor – and thereby making a statement which is a peculiar combination of tight control and wild randomness, the promptings of the unconscious given shape and logic by the craftsman's close attention. Of course, these observations are true of other forms of imaginative writing, but nonsense foregrounds the conjunction of tight control and lack of control more effectively than any other literary mode or genre. It's akin to the sketchpad doodle, where a random line is shaped by the artist's skill into the grotesque or elegant human or animal form which it inadvertently evokes, or where a carefully sketched conventional figure is transformed into a chimera, perhaps as a result of an initial slip of the artist's hand. In both the doodle and the nonsense poem or story, meaning arises from meaninglessness in unexpected but delightful configurations, surprising the artist as much as the reader. In the process, a kind of philosophy emerges, a way of seeing the world which is tangential to (and sometimes the reverse of) the social and moral conventions that are supposed to shape our lives.

Each accomplished writer's form of nonsense is unique. Faced with a random scribble on the page, every artist will see something different in it, just as different people see different pictures in a Rorschach blot. In response, each artist will develop a different aspect of the doodle in ways that express his or her own impulses and obsessions. As we have seen, Peake nearly always wrote the word 'nonsense' with a *c* in it – nonsence – which implies that he was well aware of its difference from the kinds perpetrated by Carroll or Lear. We have also seen that he considered it a distinct species of writing from his serious poetry: his 'divine lunacy' occupies clearly labelled notebooks of its own, and one should add that it has what one might call a dominant metre. As the Introduction to the *Collected Poems* points out, the default metre for Peake's serious poems was the iambic pentameter, the ten-syllable line deployed by Shakespeare, Milton and Tennyson. For the nonsense verse, by contrast – despite its immense metrical variety – the default metre is the iambic tetrameter, a line with four stresses, usually made up of seven or eight syllables. Often this alternates with the iambic trimeter, a three-stressed, usually six-syllable line, as in the poem 'I Must Begin to Comprehend' (p. 122):

   I must begin to comprehend
   My loves, because of my

Disorganised desire to live
Before it's time to die.

This is the so-called 'common metre' widely deployed in hymns and ballads, the forms that bring together two of Peake's strongest influences: his childhood among missionaries in China and his fascination with the sea. (Given their origin in song, it is not surprising that his nonsense verse should have been set to music by several composers.) Peake knew dozens of hymns and was always singing them, a habit he shares with the protagonist of his novel *Mr Pye* (1953). This tells the story of a self-appointed missionary who brings the good news of his own peculiar deity, the 'Great Pal', to the tiny island of Sark in the English Channel. Mr Pye has a special fondness for three hymns written partly in the 'common metre': 'Dare to Be a Daniel', 'All Things Bright and Beautiful' and 'Who Would True Valour See', and he eventually recites a nonsense poem of his own in the same metre, one of several he once wrote, he tells us, during dull board meetings 'while others doodled'. For Mr Pye, such compositions are ideally suited to times when one feels powerless and tongue-tied. He recites his verses to a small group of friends at a point when he is locked in a solitary struggle between the saintly and diabolic aspects of his personality – when wings and horns keep sprouting from his body, betokening an inward combat whose outcome neither he nor anyone else seems able to influence. 'Words at such times,' he says, 'make little sense and what sense they do make is nonsense.' The poem he declaims, 'O'er Seas that Have No Beaches' (p. 167 in this edition) is, despite its absurdity, an astonishingly eloquent evocation of loneliness, a lament for a naturally buoyant soul adrift on a shoreless ocean without hope of rescue.

It is also a song about the sea, and its subject, as well as its form, connects it with the ballad tradition, which is rich in maritime narratives, from 'Sir Patrick Spens' to 'The House Carpenter' – to say nothing of *The Ancient Mariner*, which Peake illustrated in 1943. The logic of ballads is akin to that of nonsense, with its perpetual shying away from explanations based on conventional notions of cause and effect, and its sudden unheralded obtrusions of the fantastic into the everyday. Peake's fascination with the sea was evident in his lifelong devotion to Robert Louis Stevenson's *Treasure Island*, which he also illustrated in the 1940s and could recite by heart as a boy. The sea keeps breaking into his nonsense verse, from the waters that implicitly fill the poet's brain in 'About

My Ebb- and Flow-ziness' (p. 42), and the hake-filled ocean where 'The Frivolous Cake' flees the unwanted attentions of a lustful knife (pp. 44–5), to the breakers that crash on the rhubarb-covered shoreline of 'White Mules at Prayer' (pp. 124–6), or the 'sneezing sea' to which the melancholy wanderers stray in 'Sensitive, Seldom and Sad' (p. 106). As Lear and Carroll knew – think of 'The Owl and the Pussy Cat' or the Mock Turtle – the vast pathlessness of the ocean is the perfect medium for nonsense, permitting the imagination to unmoor itself and drift at the behest of the little verbal breezes that fill its sails. But Peake's oceans are always invading the space of the domestic, carrying off random items of furniture or offering a welcome escape-route from household crises and abortive romances. Just as the sea-adventure *Treasure Island* can be found on the shelves of the most landlocked family household, so a whale finds its way onto a mantelpiece in 'It Makes a Change' (p. 88). A table of 'rare design' transports a husband and wife round an unknown archipelago in 'All Over the Lilac Brine!' (p. 78), a sofa finds itself afloat in 'O'er Seas that Have No Beaches', and a disappointed lover swims to the Arctic in 'Mine Was the One' (p. 65), where he is joined by one of the outraged brothers of 'The Ballad of Sweet Pighead', who flees to the Arctic floes to escape the disgrace of a literally pigheaded sister (p. 116). In Peake's nonsense, the cross-fertilization of the domestic setting where hymns are sung and the unstable decks to which salt-water ballads pay tribute testifies to the ineffable strangeness of families, whether these consist of childless couples or extended circles thronged with more or less distant relatives, flung into the same boat, so to speak, by the haphazard circumstances of kinship by blood or marriage.

You can choose your friends, the saying goes, but not your relatives – or even your lovers – and Peake's characters are constantly being surprised by their bizarre connections, whether with uncles, sisters, children, aunts or spouses. Uncles and aunts are especially wayward family members in Peake's universe. From the irrepressible Uncle Paul who plays the piano to his cats in 'My Uncle Paul of Pimlico' (p. 86) to the ancient aunts 'who live on sphagnum moss' in 'Crown Me with Hairpins' (p. 220), the siblings of one's parents in the nonsense verse seem helplessly in thrall to their strange addictions. The most famous of Peake's verses that take families as their subject – 'Aunts and Uncles' (pp. 150–3) – sees a succession of the titular relatives transformed into what they are obsessed by or compared with, finding the range of available

7

options for action severely curtailed by their transformations. Aunty Grace, turned into a flatfish, 'all but vanished' when seen from the side; Uncle Wog, trapped in canine form, hides himself for shame – and starts hiding bones, too, compulsively; Aunty Vi, changed to an insect, is mercilessly battered by (of all people) her favourite nephew. (One wonders if he had *always* taken advantage of her favouritism to metaphorically batter her.) These presumably unmarried and childless family members (at least, one seldom hears of spouses or offspring in connection with these aunts and uncles) have become defined by the things their nephews and nieces say about them, locked into the limited frame of reference provided by teasing, rumour and gossip; and most of them seem either indifferent to or positively delighted by the fantastic metamorphoses to which they have been subjected.

'Aunts and Uncles' illustrates one of the ways in which Peake's nonsense steers its wayward course. A string of similes or metaphors, some familiar, some unexpected, is given corporeal form in the aunts and uncles of the title, and clichés are thereby brought alive, made endlessly fruitful, so that one can imagine the series of relatives and of stanzas extending indefinitely, so jaunty is the rhythm of the poem, so amusing the antics of its cast. Some of the questions to which the series seems to respond are these: when you call your aunt a pig, snake, cold fish, or insect, what are you doing to her, and how might she react to being so labelled? If she took the comparison to heart, or became what you called her, how might she adapt her domestic arrangements to the needs of her new identity? There's an impeccable logic to each relative's response to his or her transformation, as there is to the reactions of Gregor Samsa's family to his transformation into a beetle in Franz Kafka's *Metamorphosis*. Unlike Gregor, these eccentrics and their families take each outlandish situation in their stride, though, recognizing perhaps that the quirks of language ensure we all inhabit a universe full of incongruities and inexplicable changes, to which we adapt ourselves every second of our lives without noticing our own versatility.

Conversations offer constant examples of this versatility, as we respond from moment to moment to the misunderstandings that bedevil our efforts at communication. Many of Peake's most elaborate nonsense verses take the form of dialogues at cross purposes, from the fatal exchange between the tigerish 'confidential stranger' and his victim in 'Come, Sit Beside Me Dear, He Said' (pp. 60–1) to the inconclusive chat between a singing giraffe and a woman in 'Deliria' (pp. 63–4), or the squabble between husband and wife in 'Come Husband! Come, and Ply the Trade' (pp. 69–71). The wandering paths taken by these dialogues are lent their mazy complexity by the failure of either party to fathom the desires or intentions of his or her interlocutor; a failure that finds its most vivid expression in the heroine's terror of Figures of Speech in 'It Worries Me to Know' (pp. 161–5). Locutions such as 'You have blood on your hands' haunt this heroine like vengeful ghosts, recalling for her some unspecified 'crime / I did when I was three' and hampering her efforts to articulate her fears to the 'wise and cloudy man' who seeks to advise her. For her, Figures of Speech are malignant things, prone to ambushing their users – as happens when the old man leaves her to 'hold the floor' at the end of the poem, which gives her blisters on both hands from gripping the parquet. In the end the heroine retreats to pastoral seclusion, although even here the mooing of cows leads her to speculate about their inward life. The Figures of Speech have been too vigorously suggestive for her, driving her to take flight from conversation altogether, like many of the protagonists of Peake's narratives in prose and verse. Their dangerous vitality is gloriously captured in the series of drawings Peake produced for a book, *Figures of Speech*, in 1954, which we have used as illustrations in this edition, because of their obvious affinity with 'It Worries Me to Know', and because they are the visual counterpart to Peake's habit of literalizing metaphor in his poetry and prose.

In Peake's nonsense, similes and Figures of Speech unspool threads of ideas or images that develop into elaborate stories or quasi-dramatic exchanges; and threads themselves are one of the many repeated themes that run through his nonsense verse. 'The Threads of Thought Are Not for Me' (p. 68) contains no thread of thought linking its stanzas except the thought of thread itself – the cotton twine of the first stanza, the needlework of the saddle in the third, the trailing clew in the last – as if to demonstrate the capacity of the human mind to stitch things together quite independently of the causes and effects privileged in formal discourse. Threads also put in an appearance in 'The Threads Remain' (p. 123) and 'Squat Ursula' (pp. 138–9). Other obsessions are malicious bowler hats that threaten to enslave their owners ('Ode to a Bowler' (p. 30), 'Tintinnabulum' (pp. 128–37), 'The Men in Bowler Hats Are Sweet' (p. 148)); roots ('Ancient Root O Ancient Root' (p. 44), 'The Hideous Root' (pp. 140–4), 'Undertakers' Song 1' (p. 181)); horses ('I Married Her in Green' (p. 50), 'The Threads of Thought' (p. 68),

'The Osseous 'Orse' (p. 154), 'Come, Break the News to Me, Sweet Horse!' (pp. 200–1)), and a menagerie of other animals. These thematic threads bind the nonsense verse together much as references to Jubjub birds and the Chankly Bore bind together the nonsense verse of Carroll and Lear. What makes Peake's verse distinctive, however, is his tendency to return to the same nonsense poem or sequence of lines over many years, pursuing the imaginative possibilities it throws out in different directions each time he revisits it. For this reason we found ourselves, in this edition, printing rival versions of a number of poems because there seemed no reason to give one version precedence over another. 'Simple, Seldom and Sad' (p. 47) and 'Sensitive, Seldom and Sad' (p. 106) were clearly regarded by Peake as different poems, since he printed the latter in *Rhymes Without Reason* (1944) and the former two years later in *Titus Groan* (1946), despite having (apparently) written it first. 'Deliria' (pp. 63–4) is a different poem from 'The Camel' (p. 96); both versions of 'How Good It Is to Be Alone' (pp. 71–3) and of 'The Sunlight Lies upon the Fields' / 'The Sunlight Falls Upon the Grass' (pp. 64 and 80) have something distinctive to recommend them; and 'I Must Begin to Comprehend' (p. 122) and 'The Threads Remain' (p. 123) has each its own atmosphere, despite the number of lines they have in common. The lines 'Half tragical, half magical, / And half an hour, or two' occur in both of the latter poems as well as in 'What a Day It's Been!' (p. 90), which Peake published in *Rhymes without Reason* three years or so before inscribing 'The Threads Remain' in his 1947 notebook. Each pair of poems or duplicated lines, whether placed side by side in this edition or separated by several pages, gives us the pleasure of noting the different sorts of 'nowhere' to which nonsense can lead us from the same starting point – or how it can lead us to the same 'nowhere' from different points of origin. The journeys of nonsense extend over time as well as space, and are thus interwoven with the personal history of writers and readers as inseparably as the poems in this book are interwoven with the calamitous events of the Second World War and its aftermath.

Unlike the serious poems, Peake's nonsense verse makes no reference to contemporary historical events – with the notable exception of the fragment 'Thank God for a Tadpole' (p. 42), which is carefully dated 28 August 1939 (and is not exactly nonsense). It could be said, though, that this very rejection of its times by the nonsense verse is a kind of engagement with them. Many of the poems here concern themselves with resistance to entrapment:

whether successful, as when the protagonist of 'Tintinnabulum' casts aside his soul-destroying bowler, or when Sweet Pighead decides to defy popular prejudice against her appearance with 'unflinching courage'; or unsuccessful, as when the 'healthy, happy man' Footfruit is converted to dismal conformity with the 'civilization' of capitalism, and reduced to wretched ill-health in the process. Peake's nonsense, like the other products of his imagination, is an act of defiance against the violence of war, the market forces that made his existence as an artist so tenuous, and the affectations and double standards of middle-class life, with which he seems to have had a love–hate relationship not unlike the feeling Titus has for the stifling ritual of Gormenghast castle in Peake's most celebrated works, the Titus novels.

This brings us to what is perhaps the most intriguing aspect of the nonsense verse: its affinity with the adventures of Titus Groan. Nonsense verse is the poetry of Gormenghast – the massive, self-sufficient fortress which stands at the heart of the Titus novels, and which casts its shadow over the hero of the sequence long after he has shaken its dust from his feet and set out for the wilderness of factories, parties, zoos and homeless shelters that lies beyond. It's nonsense verse that Titus's sister Fuchsia reads in her secret attic hideaway, taking refuge in its triumphant non-compliance with the unbending ritual that governs her life as a daughter of the House of Groan. It's nonsense verse that Titus's father, Lord Sepulchrave, spouts when his library is burned to the ground by the upstart Steerpike, an atrocity that drives the book-loving Earl to madness and death. It's nonsense verse that the Castle Poet intones when he pokes his head out unexpectedly from one of the windows of the ancient fastness, like an animated fragment of its architecture. Later, in the third of the Titus books, in which the young protagonist escapes from the castle and finds himself wandering a landscape full of capitalists, self-servers, vagrants and rebels, every part of his new environment seems to possess its own peculiar brand of nonsense poetry. The Titus books could in fact be described as an extended meditation on nonsense and the unique perspective on the world it lends us – the many uses to which it may be put, as various as the uses to which surrealism and other avant-garde forms were being co-opted in the artistic milieu of the 1940s and 1950s.

Just how central nonsense verse is to the castle is made clear at the end of *Gormenghast* when the Castle Poet takes on the role of Master of Ritual: custodian, that is, of the giant books that contain the only authoritative record of the complex and crazy rituals by which the castle community is regulated. The poem this Poet recites on his first appearance in *Titus Groan*, 'Linger Now with Me, Thou Beauty' (pp. 48–9 in this book), marks him out as an indolent 'wastrel' who takes no account of time or the castle's economy, rapt in perpetual contemplation of his own aimless verses ('the splendour / Of [his] vision') and of his desire for an unidentified 'Love' to share them with. By taking on the mantle of Master of Ritual, the Poet ensures that other wastrels will be able to go on leading an equally aimless existence. This is because despite the byzantine, pointless rituals that control it – or perhaps *because* of them – Gormenghast constitutes a haven for those who seek shelter from the remorseless logic of the world outside: a logic that led to war, genocide, book-burning, and the brutal monotony of army life during the years when Peake was writing the first of the Titus novels, *Titus Groan*, between 1941 and 1946. The castle's attics, staircases and crumbling archways offer abundant secret spaces where the likes of Fuchsia, Titus and the Poet may construct their imaginative worlds: little self-contained visual or verbal bubbles, which resolutely refuse all connection with the environment in which they are fashioned, whether Gormenghast itself or the war-torn Britain that gave it birth. Poetry is as much a part of Gormenghast's ritual as it is of the individual lives of its inhabitants. The masque figure of a Horse reads from a book of poems during the public celebration of Titus's tenth birthday. Dr Prunesquallor reads in his study from a book of poems written by Fuchsia in an exercise book that closely resembles the nonsense notebooks we described at the beginning of this Introduction. Sometimes the poems are inscribed in a 'heavy, ponderous and childish hand – sometimes in a quick, excited calligraphy, full of crossings-out and misspellings', just like Peake's own manuscripts. It's as if Gormenghast were the one space in which Peake's works could be wholly at home, a safe house from the various conflicts beyond its boundaries, and from the marketplace where his poetic and artistic visions were all too often seen as self-indulgent irrelevances.

Among Fuchsia's verses, one in particular catches Prunesquallor's eye, 'How White and Scarlet Is that Face' (p. 157), in which she confesses her fascination with the deadly Steerpike. The fact that the poem refers to something outside itself – like Peake's poem 'Thank God for a Tadpole' – signals the threat that Steerpike poses to the castle, whose identity, like that of the nonsense verse it nurtures, depends on its self-sufficiency, its resistance to the forces of the marketplace or the dictator's podium. Steerpike first enters Fuchsia's life in *Titus Groan* when he climbs into her attic refuge and reads a nonsense poem there – 'Sensitive, Seldom and Sad' – while munching on a half-eaten pear he finds beside it. The poem gives him an insight into Fuchsia's psychology, and he uses this insight to begin the long process of seducing her; a process that ends in *Gormenghast* with Fuchsia's suicide, when she realizes that the man she had thought of as a poet – who wooed her with poems, perhaps plagiaristic of the nonsense verses he read in her attic – is in fact a sadistic murderer and would-be totalitarian despot, an infiltrator from the nightmarish 'real' world of the 1940s.

We are not permitted to read all the nonsense poetry we hear about in the Titus books. The verses spouted by the Horse at Titus's birthday party remain inaudible to the reader; of Fuchsia's poems we read only the one about Steerpike; and when Fuchsia refuses to hear Steerpike's last poem to her we lose the chance to judge his skill as a ventriloquist, aping the kinds of rhymes that are closest to her heart. In this edition, however, you will find several poems that never found their way into the published pages of Peake's great sequence. The song promised by the chef Swelter to his apprentices, which he never sings, is here in its entirety ('Swelter's Song', pp. 53–6). So is the lullaby sung to the keeper of the Hall of the Bright Carvings, Rottcodd, by his mother ('White Mules at Prayer', pp. 124–6); and a lascivious lyric declaimed by the Castle Poet to the Countess of Groan ('Song of the Castle Poet', p. 156). The ballad 'It Worries Me to Know' recalls the relationship between the schoolmaster Bellgrove and Irma Prunesquallor in the second Titus novel and ends with a seeming allusion to the flood that closes it ('All these and many more float past / Across the roofs of Gormenghast', p. 165). There are three songs sung by Nannie Slagg to the infant Titus in a radio adaptation of *Titus Groan*, as well as a lyric for Fuchsia from the same source (pp. 183–4). Nonsense verse is the poetry of Gormenghast; but lovers of the Titus books will find here a great deal more than those novels, fine as they are, will have prepared them for. We hope you enjoy the adventure of reading them as much as we enjoyed the adventure of seeking them out.

R.W. Maslen
2011

A Note on the Text

This edition was compiled under rather unusual circumstances. In February 2010, after months of negotiation, Sebastian Peake succeeded in acquiring the rights to the material contained in Mervyn Peake's *Book of Nonsense*, which he planned to include in an edition of his father's collected nonsense. (It is a testament to the enduring popularity of these poems that *A Book of Nonsense* has remained in print for nearly forty years.) Sebastian naturally hoped to see the new edition prepared in time for the centenary of Peake's birth in 2011. The problem was that the entire Peake archive – all the documents preserved by the Peake family relating to Mervyn Peake's career as novelist, playwright and poet – was at that point being held by Sotheby's in Bond Street, awaiting collection by the British Library, which had just bought it for the nation. Once at the Library, the papers would not be accessible until cataloguing and preservation were complete, sometime in mid-2011. From the moment when Sebastian obtained the rights to *A Book of Nonsense* there was about a fortnight before the Library took possession of the papers; not much time for exhaustive quarrying of the archive. After discussing the situation with Peter Selley of Sotheby's, Sebastian arranged for Rob Maslen to travel to London and consult the Peake papers in Sotheby's Bond Street office, where in the end he spent only two full days checking the accuracy of the published nonsense verse against the original manuscripts and discovering new, unpublished verses for inclusion in the edition. Since that time, both editors have scrupulously checked the texts of all the poems of which they have copies or for which there exist authoritative printed versions proof-read by Peake himself, but we have been unable to re-check the material unique to the Peake archive while it was being catalogued and conserved by the British Library. Any inaccuracies or omissions in our transcriptions will be corrected, we trust, in future editions of this volume. In the meantime we can only assure readers that we have done our very best to provide the most accurate texts we could in the time available.

Original punctuation and spelling have been preserved throughout, except where this was thought to make Peake's sense (or nonsense) difficult to follow. Punctuation has occasionally been added and some obvious errors corrected, for the same reason. All editorial amendments have been recorded in the Notes.

References and Further Reading

Listed below are all the editions, criticism and biographies cited in the notes, along with other texts we have found helpful in writing the Introduction and thinking about Peake's nonsense. For a full list consult the Peake bibliography on the website of *Peake Studies* (http://peakestudies.com/contents.htm). This includes an authoritative 'Title and First-Line Index to Peake's Poems'.

Editions are listed in chronological order. Unless otherwise indicated, the place of publication is London.

Editions of Peake's Work

Ride a Cock-horse (Chatto and Windus, 1940)
Shapes and Sounds (Chatto and Windus, 1941)
Rhymes Without Reason (Eyre and Spottiswoode, 1944)
Titus Groan (Eyre and Spottiswoode, 1946)
Letters from a Lost Uncle (from Polar Regions) (Eyre and Spottiswoode, 1948)
The Glassblowers (Eyre and Spottiswoode, 1950)
Gormenghast (Eyre and Spottiswoode, 1950)
Mr Pye (Heinemann, 1953)
'Alice and Tenniel and Me', radio talk, *The Listener*, 23 December 1953 (incomplete); the full text was printed in *The Mervyn Peake Review*, no. 6 (Spring 1978), pp. 20–24
Figures of Speech (Gollancz, 1954)
Titus Alone (Eyre and Spottiswoode, 1959; second English edition (revised), 1970)
The Rhyme of the Flying Bomb (Dent, 1960)
A Book of Nonsense (Peter Owen, 1972)
The Drawings of Mervyn Peake (Davis Poynter, 1974)
Writings and Drawings, ed. Maeve Gilmore and Shelagh Johnson (London and New York: Academy Editions/St Martin's Press, 1974)
Peake's Progess, ed. Maeve Gilmore (Allen Lane, 1978; first paper-

back edition with corrections by G. Peter Winnington, Harmondsworth: Penguin, 1981). Contains Peake's plays *The Wit to Woo* (performed 1957) and *Noah's Ark* (not yet performed)
Collected Poems, ed. R.W. Maslen, Fyfield Books (Manchester: Carcanet, 2008)
Manifold Basket (unfinished play), ed. G. Peter Winnington, *Peake Studies*, vol. 11, no. 2 (April 2009), pp. 3–32

Biographies and Memoirs

Batchelor, John, *Mervyn Peake: A Biographical and Critical Exploration* (Duckworth, 1974)
Gilmore, Maeve, *A World Away: A Memoir of Mervyn Peake* (Gollancz, 1970)
Peake, Sebastian, *A Child of Bliss: Growing Up with Mervyn Peake* (Oxford: Lennard, 1989)
Smith, Gordon, *Mervyn Peake: A Personal Memoir* (Gollancz, 1984)
Winnington, G. Peter, *Vast Alchemies: The Life and Work of Mervyn Peake* (London and Chester Springs: Peter Owen, 2000); second edition (revised), retitled *Mervyn Peake's Vast Alchemies: The Illustrated Biography* (2009)
— (ed.), *Mervyn Peake: The Man and his Art* (London and Chester Springs, PA: Peter Owen, 2006)
Yorke, Malcolm, *Mervyn Peake: My Eyes Mint Gold. A Life* (John Murray, 2000)

Criticism

Barford, Duncan, '"Madness Can Be Lovely": The Range and Meaning of Mervyn Peake's Nonsense Verse', *Peake Studies*, vol. 4, no. 1 (Autumn 1994), pp. 29–52. The most thorough critical and theoretical appreciation of Peake's nonsense to date.
Batchelor, John, *Mervyn Peake: A Biographical and Critical Exploration* (Duckworth, 1974). Chapter 6, on *Titus Groan*, has a brief mention of Peake's nonsense verse (pp. 78–9), but it is not analysed in the excellent chapter on his poetry (Chapter 10).
Betjeman, John, review of *Rhymes Without Reason*, *Daily Herald*, 13 December 1944, p. 2. Betjeman describes it as 'Quite the outstanding book I have for review… I have bought more than one copy, particularly for the last poem' (i.e. 'Sensitive, Seldom and Sad').
Le Guin, Ursula, '*Peake's Progress*, by Mervyn Peake', *Dancing at the*

Edge of the World: thoughts on Words, Women, Places (New York etc.: Harper and Row, 1989), pp. 273–5. This short but astute review recognizes the nonsense verse as being central to Peake's achievement: 'He was a master of nonsense to equal Edward Lear.'

Mills, Alice, *Stuckness in the Fiction of Mervyn Peake* (Rodopi: Amsterdam and New York, 2006). Chapter 4, 'Nonsense, Stuckness and the Abject in *Titus Groan*', pays attention to the nonsense verse.

Winnington, G. Peter, *The Voice of the Heart: The Working of Mervyn Peake's Imagination* (Liverpool: Liverpool University Press, 2006). Discusses Peake's poetry in every chapter.

Complete Nonsense

From *Figures of Speech*. The Key to the drawing is on p. 234.

I Saw a Puffin

I saw a Puffin
In the Bay of Baffin
Sittin on Nuffin
And it was Laffin.

(c. 1918)

The Song of Lien Tsung

Although you may not understand it
I've always yearned to be a bandit;
It may seem vaguely funny and it
    May of course seem more so
But now that from my love I'm taken
I'm like an egg without its bacon –
And so strange conflicts grip my shaken
    Yellow torso.

(January 1930)

Railway Ditties

Waddon

Whad'n earth would I do if I lived in Waddon?
Whad'n Earth would I do?

(c. 1930)

Thornton Heath

I always cast a Mental Wreath
Upon the Lines at Thornton Heath
In Pity for the Dead who climb
The train each morning in which I'm.

(c. 1930)

Norbury

Snobbery S'Norbury
Suffers from fobbery
Each little strawberry
Costs you a bobbery

(c. 1930)

Streatham and Balham

Oh why is Streatham Common
And Balham so élite?
Because on mats in Balham
You always wipe your feet –
While through the Halls of Streatham
One carries half the street.

(c. 1930)

Green Park

What could be greener
Than Green Park?
I've never seen-a
Park that's greener
Than Green Park!

(August 1930)

You Can Never Be Sure of Your Birron

You can never be sure of your Birron,
But of this be you blooming well sure,
A Birron is always a Birron
Enceforward, evermore.

(early 1930s)

From *Figures of Speech*. The Key to the drawing is on p. 234.

Beard of My Chin

Beard of my chin, white product of my jaw,
Pour through the dizzy height, white offshoot, pour!
Down the abyss, most fertile growth, cascade –
This precipice was for this cataract made.
Twelve thousand fathoms from this verge it is
To where below me spread the plains of Phiz.
The sunset tinges my fair growth and I
Am almost crumpled up with ecstasy.

(early 1930s)

You Before Me

You before me
Except after tea
Is my creed and my motto
(My wife calls me Otto)

(early 1930s)

Although I Love Him

Although I love him and could never find
It in my heart to chasten him, I see
No way to comprehend him, nor am blind
To his ungainly posturings at tea

(early 1930s)

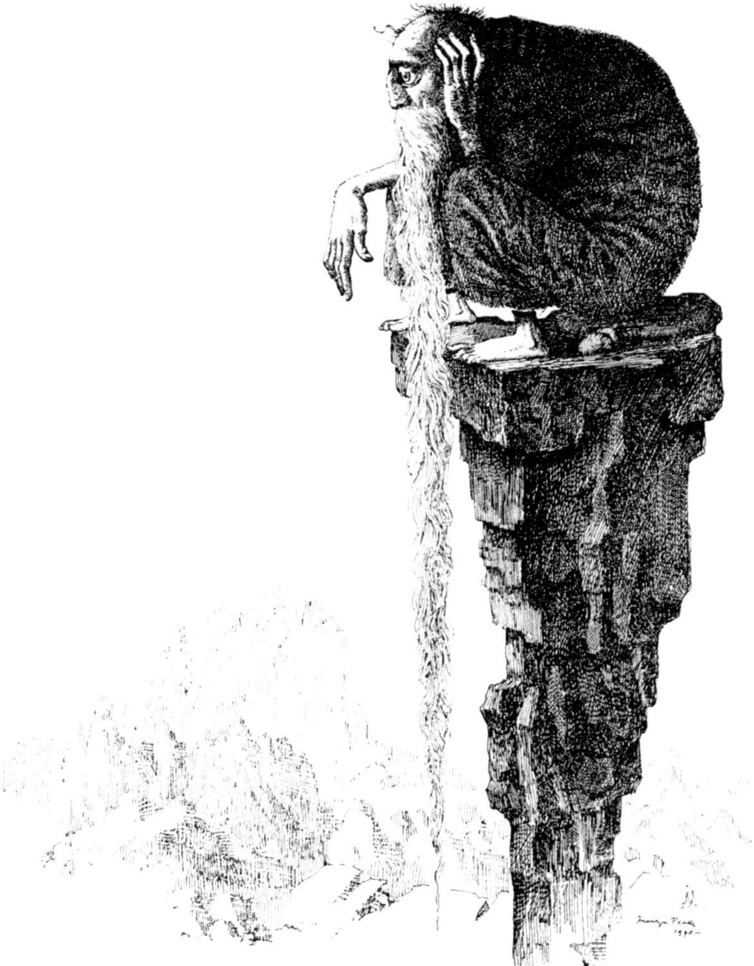

From *Figures of Speech*. The Key to the drawing is on p. 234.

Practically Poetry

He must be an artist...
    Look at his shirt!
He must be a genius...
    Look at the dirt!
My deah! How too thrilling!
    My deah! What a shriek!!
His work must be *brilliant*...
    Just *look* at his beard...
So to speak.

(December 1934)

Ode to a Bowler

Oh, Hat that cows the spirit!
　　…If any spirit be…
First cousin to the Black Cap
　　And sign of slavery!
Funereal and horrible…
　　But this at least I owe it;
It matches to a nicety
　　The Face that Sits Below It!

(December 1934)

Raft Song of the Conger Eel

Strangul'm, scragle'm
Scrunch'm
One – two and away.
Batter'm, shatter'm
Gut'm and groans
Red of the blood in the spray.
One – two,
And away.

Throttle'm, bottle'm
Cut'm a rip
Three – four and away.
Plunder'm, thunder'm
Into a ship
Red of the blood in the spray.
Five – six,
And away.

(c. 1933–6)

From *Figures of Speech*. The Key to the drawing is on p. 234.

From *Figures of Speech*. The Key to the drawing is on p. 234.

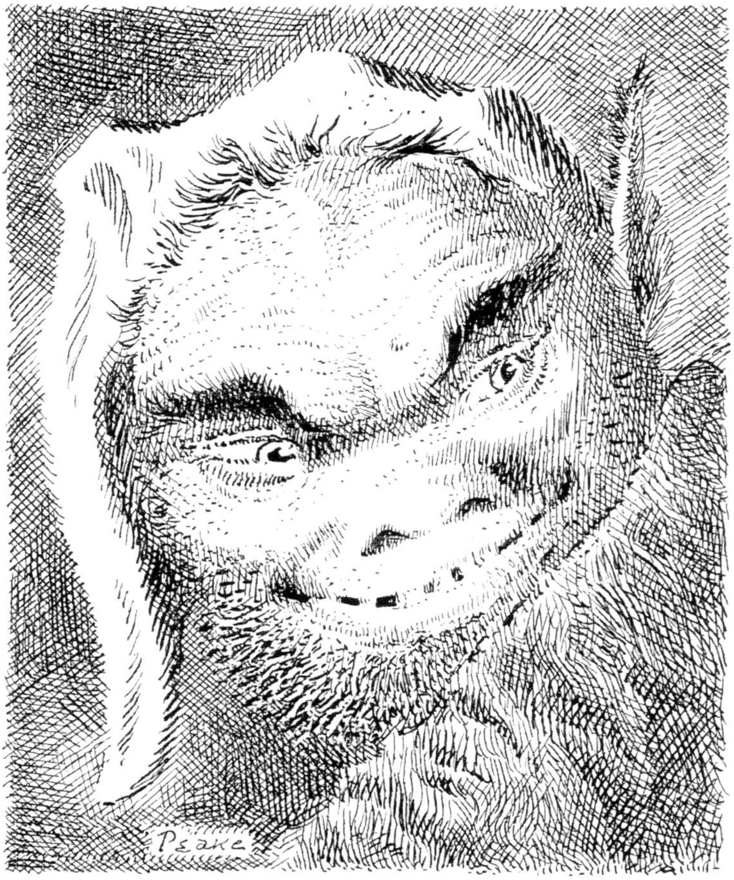
Peake

The Dwarf of Battersea

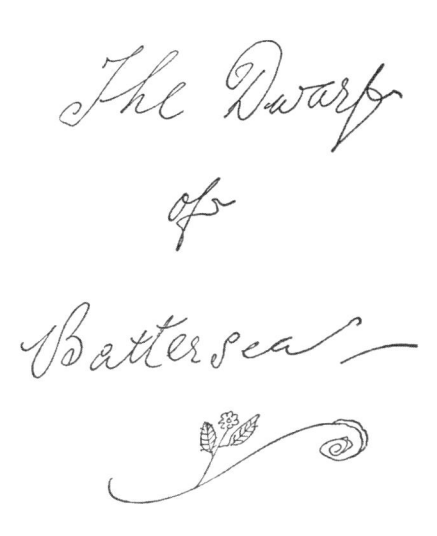

The Dwarf of Battersea

Ye olde Ballade concerning ye yellow dwarfe of Battersea
being a
true and truſtworthy account of hiſ
death
at ye hand of ye repulſive artift Master Mervyn Peake
when
defending ye gloriously beautiful and beguiling
charmer Maeve
in
the year of Our Lord 1937.

For ye benefit of preſent-day readers, ye famouse olde Ballade has been re-spelſt according to modern faſsion.

Please turn over

1.

There lived a dwarf in Battersea
(O lend me a tanner!)
There lived a dwarf in Battersea
Whose hands were white with leprosy
(Sing you-O, to me-O,)
And the river runs away.

2.

At dead of night he crept to see
(O lend me a tanner!)
At dead of night he crept to see
What he could see at 163!
(Sing you-O to me-O)
And the river rolls away.

3.

And there he saw a maiden fair
(O lend me a tanner!)
And there he saw a maiden fair
With tawny eyes and tawny hair
(Sing you-O, to me-O)
And the river runs away.

4

Then through the letterbox he crept
(O lend me a tanner!)
Then through the letter-box he crept
To where the golden lady slept.
(Sing you-O, for me-O)
And the river rolls away.

5.

He gave a most disgusting croak
(O lend me a tanner!)
He gave a most disgusting croak
At which the sleeping one awoke,
(Sing you O, for me-O)
And the river runs away.

1

There lived a dwarf in Battersea
      (O lend me a tanner!)
There lived a dwarf in Battersea
Whose hands were white with leprosy
      (Sing you-O, to me-O)
And the river runs away.

2

At dead of night he crept to see
      (O lend me a tanner!)
At dead of night he crept to see
What he could see at 163!
      (Sing you-O, to me-O)
And the river rolls away.

3

And there he saw a maiden fair
      (O lend me a tanner!)
And there he saw a maiden fair
With tawny eyes and tawny hair
      (Sing you-O, to me-O)
And the river runs away.

4

Then through the letterbox he crept
      (O lend me a tanner!)
Then through the letterbox he crept
 To where the golden lady slept
      (Sing you-O, for me-O)
And the river rolls away.

5

He gave a most disgusting croak
    (O lend me a tanner!)
He gave a most disgusting croak
At which the sleeping one awoke.
    (Sing you-O, for me-O)
And the river runs away.

6

The dwarf hissed through his pointed teeth
    (O lend me a tanner!)
The dwarf hissed through his pointed teeth
And drew a skewer from its sheath
    (Sing you-O, to me-O)
And the river rolls away.

7

But look! A creature high above
    (O lend me a tanner!)
But see! A creature high above
Has singed the yellow wall with love!
    (Sing you-O, to me-O)
And the river runs away.

8

And like the story tales of yore
    (O lend me a tanner!)
And like the story tales of yore
This creature leaps upon the floor
    (Sing you-O, to me-O)
And the river rolls away.

9

O he came sailing through the air
    (O lend me a tanner!)
O he came sailing through the air
For what man dareth he will dare
    (Sing you-O, to me-O)
And the river runs away.

10

His hair was dark his lips were fat
    (O lend me a tanner!)
His hair was dark his lips were fat
He wore a greeny yellow hat
    (Sing you-O, to me-O)
And the river rolls away.

11

He thrust a paintbrush through the dwarf
    (O lend me a tanner!)
He thrust a paintbrush through the dwarf
And shouted with a grisly larf…
    (Sing you-O, to me-O)
And the river rolls away.

12

'Get in this tin of linseed oil!'
    (O lend me a tanner!)
'Get in this tin of linseed oil
Before I put it on to boil!'
    (Sing you-O, to me-O)
And the river runs away.

13

The dwarf turned white but did as bid
    (O lend me a tanner!)
The dwarf turned white but did as bid
And then they fastened down the lid
    (Sing you-O, to me-O)
And the river runs away.

14

They danced a tango up and down
    (O lend me a tanner!)
They danced a tango up and down
Until the yellow dwarf went brown
    (Sing you-O, to me-O)
And the river rolls away.

15

Until the yellow dwarf went black
    (O lend me a tanner!)
Until the yellow dwarf went black
And then they laid him on his back
    (Sing you-O, to me-O)
And the river runs away.

16

Until the yellow dwarf went red
    (O lend me a tanner!)
Until the yellow dwarf went red
And then they stood him on his head!
    (Sing you-O, to me-O)
And the river rolls away.

17

And sent him down the Thames afloat
    (O lend me a tanner!)
And sent him down the Thames afloat
Within a papier-maché boat
    (Sing you-O, to me-O)
And the river rolls away.

18

So one and all beware who wish
     (O lend me a tanner!)
So one and all beware who wish
Within the sacred pool to fish!
     (Sing you-O, to me-O)
And the river runs away.

19

And all beware who wish to see
     (O lend me a tanner!)
And all beware who hope to see
The golden light of 163
     (Sing you-O, to me-O)
And the river rolls away!

20

There lived a dwarf in Battersea
     (O lend me a tanner!)
There lived a dwarf in Battersea
But he has now passed over see
And where is he? O don't ask me!
     (Sing you-O, to me-O)
And the river rolls away
    A way
And the river rolls away.

(1937)

Thank God for a Tadpole

Thank God for a tadpole!
At a time like this
Thank God for a tadpole
That loses its tail,
But never its head
On the foul river bed
It wiggles its tail
(But never its head)
Not a crab or a dog
Or an indian hog
But a beautiful frog

(28 August 1939)

About My Ebb and Flow-ziness

About my ebb and flow-ziness
I must conserve my brain
And live in warmth and cosiness
Until I feel the pain.
Why irritate the present tense
The past is over now!
The future hasn't come! Have sense
And let the taffrail go.

(c. 1939)

A Fair Amount of Doziness

A fair amount of doziness
Is exquisite to me
My sister's paltry nosiness
About my ebb and floziness
Of consciousness
Is obvious-
Ly arrant jealousy.

(c. 1939)

Ancient Root O Ancient Root

Ancient Root O Ancient Root
What a wild barbaric loot
Is this I claim, in finding Thee
The King of Horrible Fantasy

Ancient One, O Ancient One
Lives there aught beneath the Sun
So wrinkled, hideous, and so
Entirely unabashed, as thou?

(c. 1939)

The Frivolous Cake

A freckled and frivolous cake there was
    That sailed on a pointless sea,
Or any lugubrious lake there was
    In a manner emphatic and free.
How jointlessly, and how jointlessly
    The frivolous cake sailed by
On the waves of the ocean that pointlessly
    Threw fish to the lilac sky.

Oh, plenty and plenty of hake there was
    Of a glory beyond compare,
And every conceivable make there was
    Was tossed through the lilac air.

Up the smooth billows and over the crests
    Of the cumbersome combers flew
The frivolous cake with a knife in the wake
    Of herself and her curranty crew.
Like a swordfish grim it would bounce and skim
    (This dinner knife fierce and blue),
And the frivolous cake was filled to the brim
    With the fun of her curranty crew.

Oh, plenty and plenty of hake there was
    Of a glory beyond compare –
And every conceivable make there was
    Was tossed through the lilac air.

Around the shores of the Elegant Isles
    Where the cat-fish bask and purr
And lick their paws with adhesive smiles
    And wriggle their fins of fur,
They fly and fly 'neath the lilac sky –
    The frivolous cake, and the knife
Who winketh his glamorous indigo eye
    In the wake of his future wife.

The crumbs blow free down the pointless sea
    To the beat of a cakey heart
And the sensitive steel of the knife can feel
    That love is a race apart.
In the speed of the lingering light are blown
    The crumbs to the hake above,
And the tropical air vibrates to the drone
    Of a cake in the throes of love.

                                                  (c. 1939)

From *Figures of Speech*. The Key to the drawing is on p. 234.

Simple, Seldom and Sad

Simple, seldom and sad
      We are
Alone on the Halibut Hills
      Afar
With sweet mad Expressions
      Of old
Strangely beautiful,
      So we're told
By the Creatures that Move
      In the sky
      And Die
On the night when the Dead Trees
      Prance and Cry.

Sensitive, seldom, and sad –
Sensitive, seldom, and sad –

Simple, seldom and sad
      Are we
When we take our path
      To the purple sea –
With mad, sweet Expressions
      Of Yore,
Strangely beautiful,
      Yea, and More
On the Night of all Nights
      When the sky
      Streams by
In rags, while the Dead Trees
      Prance and Die.

Sensitive, seldom, and sad –
Sensitive, seldom, and sad.

(c. 1939)

Linger Now with Me, Thou Beauty

Linger now with me, thou Beauty,
    On the sharp archaic shore.
Surely 'tis a wastrel's duty
    And the gods could ask no more.
If thou lingerest when I linger,
    If thou tread'st the stones I tread,
Thou wilt stay my spirit's hunger
    And dispel the dreams I dread.

Come thou, love, my own, my only,
    Through the battlements of Groan;
Lingering becomes so lonely
    When one lingers on one's own.

I have lingered in the cloisters
    Of the Northern Wing at night,
As the sky unclasped its oysters
    On the midnight pearls of light.
For the long remorseless shadows
    Chilled me with exquisite fear.
I have lingered in cold meadows
    Through a month of rain, my dear.

Come, my Love, my sweet, my Only,
    Through the parapets of Groan.
Lingering can be very lonely
    When one lingers on one's own.

In dark alcoves I have lingered
    Conscious of dead dynasties.
I have lingered in blue cellars
    And in hollow trunks of trees.
Many a traveller through moonlight
    Passing by a winding stair
Or a cold and crumbling archway
    Has been shocked to see me there.

I have longed for thee, my Only,
    Hark! the footsteps of the Groan!
Lingering is so very lonely
    When one lingers all alone.

Will you come with me, and linger?
    And discourse with me of those
Secret things the mystic finger
    Points to, but will not disclose?
When I'm all alone, my glory,
    Always fades, because I find
Being lonely drives the splendour
    Of my vision from my mind.

Come, oh come, my own! my Only!
    Through the Gormenghast of Groan.
Lingering has become so lonely
    As I linger all alone!

(October 1940)

I Married Her in Green

I married her in green
I married her in pink
And when it came to yellow
I knew just what to think

I murdered her in blue
I murdered her in red
And when I came to yellow
I found that she was dead.

I buried her in black
I buried her in white
But when it came to yellow
I knew that I was right

I found a horse of leaves
With skin as bright as gorse
And when the leaves were gone
There wasn't any horse

I laugh until I'm fat
I laugh until I'm thin
And then I find a bottle
To put my dentures in

(October 1940)

From *Figures of Speech*. The Key to the drawing is on p. 234.

From *Figures of Speech*. The Key to the drawing is on p. 234.

Swelter's Song

Give me food 'n' drink 'n' fun
'N' flamingoesh of gweat pwishe,
Marshing round me eff'ry one
Of their fevvers pwink 'n' nishe.
Give me an emblashoned waishtcoat
Flowered 'n' shtarred in gween 'n' bwown
'N' a small shea-worthy pashte-boat
I can shtick to, when I dwown.

Give me theshe, cold fwend, and calloush!
They will help me wif my pwide.
What ish it that makesh you jealoush
To behold me shatishfied?

Give me a long sword that glittersh
And a drove of burnished fliesh.
Theshe will waft me into regionsh
Coveted in Paradishe.
Give me a blue pinnacle
That shtabsh into a shky of flowersh
And I'll revel in a cool
Transhendanshy for hoursh and hoursh.

Give me theshe cold fwend, 'n' bwiefly
I shall never need a bwide.
Theshe are what I long for, chiefly –
Theshe would leave me shatishfied.

'Do you appreshiate its shadnesh?' said Swelter interrupting his own song and peering down into the clouds.

Give me the autumnal weather,
Sho that I can gwieve a bit!
Give me a red woollen feather
(I have heard you weave a bit.)
Give me food 'n' drink 'n' fun
'N' a table with no legs –
Let me have a tweakle bun
Eff'ry morning wif my eggs!

Give me theshe, cold fwend, & really
There'll be nuffing I'm denied –
Theshe neshessitiesh would clearly
Leave me more than shatishfied.

Yet, if you were *bent* on shtaving
Off my qualms of hollow dearth –
If I *knew* that you were cwaving
To ashist my second birth –
I would ashk you, very shimply –
And my voice would frill with pwide,
For a shmall 'n' freckled onion
Shtranded by the ebbing tide.

Give me thish! Cold shir! I promish
I will treat it well, I cried –
Such a gift would leave me shpeechlesh
And my yearningsh shatishfied.

Swelter was sagging in upon himself like something that folds itself up for the night. The words dragged on:

I will wear it ash a pendant
Calloush fwend 'n' iron willed,
I would be in the ashendant
Fwend! Cold fwend, I'd be fulfilled!
Yet I shee you haven't altered,
You are shtill ash cold as ice
In that cashe (and here I falters)
I shall have to pway the price.

Since you will not undershtand me
(Barren twee, unfructified,
Such am I!) when you *could* hand me
All, and make me shatishfied

Swelter with Kitchen urchin

If I waive the final item
Adamantine shir! 'n' hide
My emoshions when I mish it
Dangling at my naked shide –
Shir! cold shir, if you could give me
What I asked for firshtly, I'd
Be for effermore your debtor
And be oh sho shatishfied –

Jusht perhapsh a few flamingoesh
'N' the waishtcoat gween 'n' bwown –
'N' a shmall, shea-worthy pashte-boat
I can shtick to… as… I… dwown.

(November 1940)

From *Figures of Speech*. The Key to the drawing is on p. 234.

I Cannot Simply Stand and Watch

I cannot simply stand and watch
A man of fourteen stone
Skinning his wife upon the sly
And thinking he's alone.
I always go straight up to him
And take away his knife,
Then looking in his eyes I say
'Why must you skin your wife?'

On nine times out of every ten
Two tears start from his eyes,
And if he's really genuine
He follows them with sighs
And then a kind of plaintive groan
Wracks his whole body through
Which makes me give him back his knife
And say 'Go friend, and skin your wife
I see your point of view.'

(November 1940)

Upon the Summit of a Hill

Upon the summit of a hill
A bison sat alone
And from his hairy breast came forth
The sweetest moan.
Around him flowed the evening air
That ruffled his abundant hair.

(November 1940)

Come, Sit Beside Me Dear, He Said

'Come, sit beside me dear,' he said,
'And tell me why you languish.'
The tears that started from my eyes
Were eloquent, and his surprise
Showed clearly that he understood
My spirit was in anguish.

'I am a most ambrosial man,'
He said, 'So you can tell me
Exactly what your trouble is
For I am versed in mysteries,
And I will help you if I can.
What is it that befell thee?'

I sat, as I was bid, beside
The confidential stranger.
'O nothing has befallen me,'
I said, as I looked up to see
The kind of face he had, for I'd
No wish to be in danger.

He had a tiger's face, for which
I wasn't quite prepared,
And when he saw that I had seen
What I had seen, his face I mean,
He uttered a tigerian cry
And every tooth was bared.

What with the sorrow of my own
And then the disillusion!
That such a dear, soft spoken thing
Should be a beast about to spring –
I must confess my marrow-bone
Was covered with confusion.

I did *so* want to bare my heart
To someone mild as Moses
And my advice is this, that you
Should watch the face that speaks to you
Before it even speaks, and make
A thorough diagnosis.

No never listen first, then look
But always look, then listen
If you can trust the countenance –
If not, regain your feet and bounce
Across each forest field or brook
Away from what has talked to you
As fast as you can hasten.

No one has ever heard the woe
And travail that I suffered.
But now, with no solidity
I'm just a memory to me
And I could kill myself to know
What easy prey I offered.

As you have guessed, that gentleman
Has thrived on my nutrition.
He's eaten me, and I am dead,
But *do* remember what I've said:
A gentle voice may be misplaced
With a gross disposition.

(c. 1940)

From *Figures of Speech*. The Key to the drawing is on p. 234.

Deliria

I watched a camel sit astride
A rainbow in the Spring.
His eyes and legs were crossed; his hide
Was of the finest string.

The rainbow light upon his twine
Had set it all aglow
With pride and tinctures as divine
As one could wish to know.

He edged along the slender arc,
And then he rolled his eyes.
Below him the sepulchral dark
Surged through his hairy thighs;

Then, most precariously, I saw
Him stretch his length; his Vast
Expensive humps swung idly, for
He used elastoplast.

Ah, how precariously! he lay
Full length upon his hide,
While on his face such smiles made play,
As switch from side to side.

And then – he sang! but as his voice
Was very far removed,
I first mistook it for the noise
Of those whom once I loved.

'Deliria! Deliria!'
(What else could sound so sweet?)
'Deliria! Deliria!'
I heard the voice repeat.

'Deliria! Deliria!'
The haunting message came;
But I had hoped he'd tell me more
Than just my Christian name.

'Deliria! Deliria!'
Oh I grew desperate –
To hear my name, and hear no more,
So I screamed out 'Repeat

My Christian name once more to me
And I shall scorn you there,
And leave you, and go home to tea,
And brush my yellow hair.

And read my books, and never see
Or think of you again!'
I gulped, and gripped a nearby tree,
And waited in the rain.

Then through the April air, I stole
Another glance – he sat
Bolt upright on the rainbow; all
My hopes were based on that.

(1944)

The Sunlight Lies Upon the Fields

The sunlight lies upon the fields
It lies upon the trees
It lies upon the hills and clouds
And on the flowers and fleas.

It lies on everything it can,
For that is how it's made.
And it would lie on me, except
That I am in the shade.

(1944)

Mine Was the One

Mine was the One. Mine was the two;
Mine was the three and four:
And I would even say that she
Rose up to seven or more.

But she is dead; the trumpeteer
Could not agree with her,
For he was twice as much as she
Could have accounted for.

'Alack! alay! Alay, alack!
Pass me the wine; I think
The hour has come for men like me
To swim into the drink.'

He swam for many years; his friends
Last saw him thrashing far
Into those moonlit waves that freeze
Along the polar bar.

The thunder rolls across lit seas,
That bubble at the brim,
And he is swimming still, unless
A shark has eaten him.

(1944)

From *Figures of Speech*. The Key to the drawing is on p. 234.

From *Figures of Speech*. The Key to the drawing is on p. 234.

The Threads of Thought Are Not for Me

The threads of thought are not for me
But cotton ones I love,
The sort that stretch too high below,
And far too low above.

It is a case of nutriment
(A fallacy of course)
But why waste your accoutrement
On someone else's horse?

The bridle and the reins are yours,
(And most expensive too)
The needle-work, a hideous red,
The saddle, black-and-blue.

It was a most ambrosial job
(The riding of the beast)
Especially through a brandy mob
Led by a whisky priest.

Yet all this while, the rankling thought
Keeps rankling in my mind
Why suffer a promiscuous Thread
To stretch so far behind?

(1944)

Come Husband! Come, and Ply the Trade

She.
Come Husband! Come, and ply the trade
Your father handed down –
I've heard you say your brains were made
For more than half-a-crown.

He.
You flatter me, but I am weary
Of my father's trade;
And now he's dead, I'm really very
Happy I'm afraid!

She.
Come come! you cannot so dispose
Of all your father's toil
To build a business, goodness knows
He left it on the boil.

He.
I know, I know – but I prefer
To forge my own career –
So leave me if you please, or stir
My coffee for me dear.

She.
You always were pig-headed – you
He loved and stinted for!
Unkind and thoughtless husband! who
D'you think he minted for?

He.
For me of course. But don't you see
I'm made for something more
Than 'Use a rubber housemaid, we
Will bring her to your door.'

From *Figures of Speech*. The Key to the drawing is on p. 234.

She.
Conceited and ungrateful spouse,
I'm tired to death of you.
And what is more I hate this house
You built and brought me to.

He.
And you forget, sweet Irritant,
That everything about you
Reminds me that I might have spent
The last twelve years without you.

Your pear shaped head, your crimson ears,
Your eyes like bits of glass,
Your frocks cut out with garden shears
Your tooth of burnished brass.

She.
And you forget, there comes a point
When insults cease to give
Effect, and your abuse disjoints
What arguments you have.

(1944)

How Good It Is to Be Alone (1)

How good it is to be alone
With uncles and with aunts,
With nephews on the telephone
And nieces dressed like plants.

How welcome is this solitude,
With grandpa on the tray
And grandma being deaf and rude
At any time of day.

How porous and how recondite
Are peaceful days and slow.
I love my relatives to fight
For half an hour or so.

But though my thoughts are chiefly tied
To homely things and mild
I have a somewhat grimmer side,
That must be reconciled.

For sometimes, at the breathless crack
Of midnight I arise,
And floating limply on my back
I startle the wide eyes

Of relatives convulsed with cramp
To see my body wheeling
So limply round and round each lamp
That dangles from each ceiling.

Then down I swoop, all bonelessly,
And as they bridle up,
I strike them quiltwards with the cry
Of a shrill buttercup.

Ah yes! but only now and then,
When, just to vaunt my pride
And prove myself to be a man
Who *has* 'another side'.

For mostly I sit all alone
With uncles and with aunts
And nephews on the telephone
And nieces dressed like plants.

(1944)

How Good It Is to Be Alone (2)

How good it is to be alone
With uncles, and with aunts
Both underdone and overgrown
And dressed like Indian plants.

How welcome is the solitude
With grandpa on the tray,
And grandma being pink and rude
At any time of day.

How porous and how recondite
Are peaceful days and slow
'Dear children won't you scratch and bite
An extra hour or so.'

Sequestered in a chair of green
With Homer on my knee,
Sweet Relatives, I've *never* been
So full of Love for Thee.

(1944)

From *Figures of Speech*. The Key to the drawing is on p. 234.

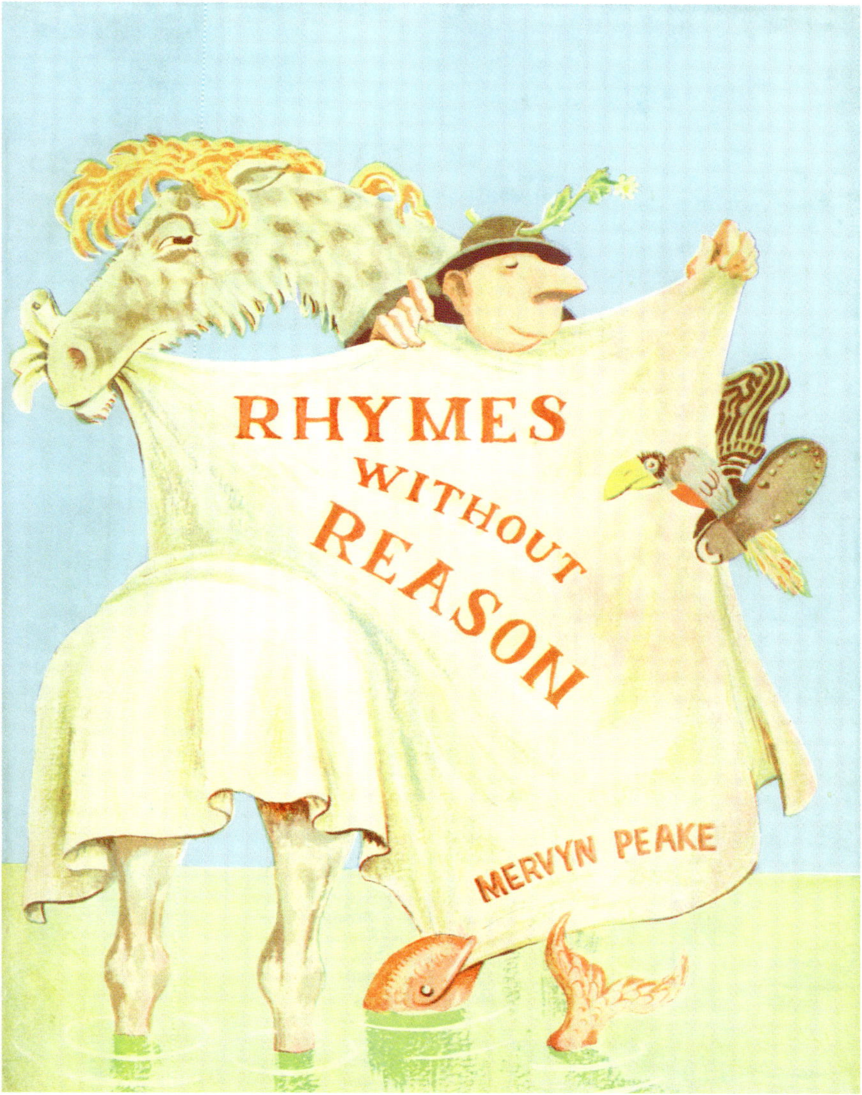
RHYMES
WITHOUT
REASON
MERVYN PEAKE

Upon My Golden Backbone

Upon my golden backbone
    I float like any cork,
That hasn't yet been washed ashore
    Or swallowed by a shark.

I never seem to want to snarl
    In jungles all day long –
I've been so much upon my back
    My legs aren't very strong.

It's all because a Pelican
I *didn't* eat one day,
Decided to look after me
    That I behave this way.

And so, while Other Tigers slink
    From tree… to tree… to tree,
I lie upon my back, and blink,
    In Aqueous Ecstasy.

(1944)

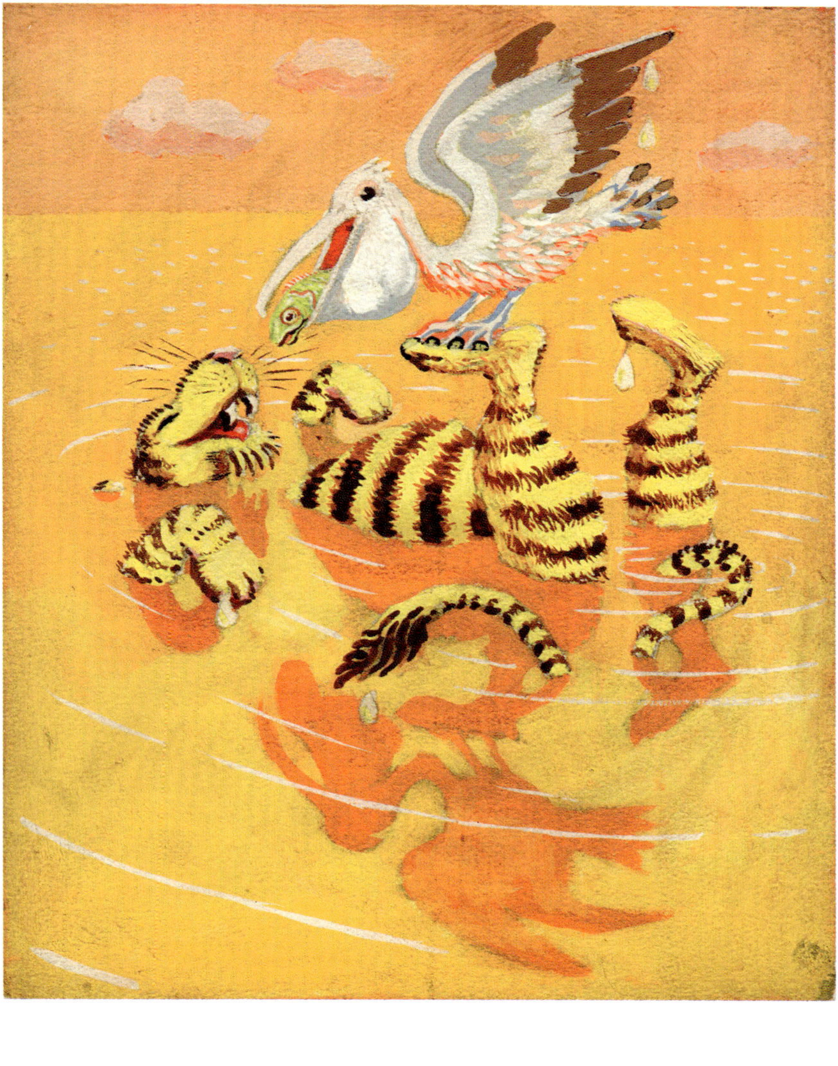

All Over the Lilac Brine!

Around the shores of the Arrogant Isles,
    Where the Cat-fish bask and purr,
And lick their paws with adhesive smiles,
    And wriggle their fins of fur,

With my wife in a dress of mustard-and-cress,
    On a table of rare design,
We skim and we fly, 'neath a fourpenny sky,
    All over the lilac brine.

(1944)

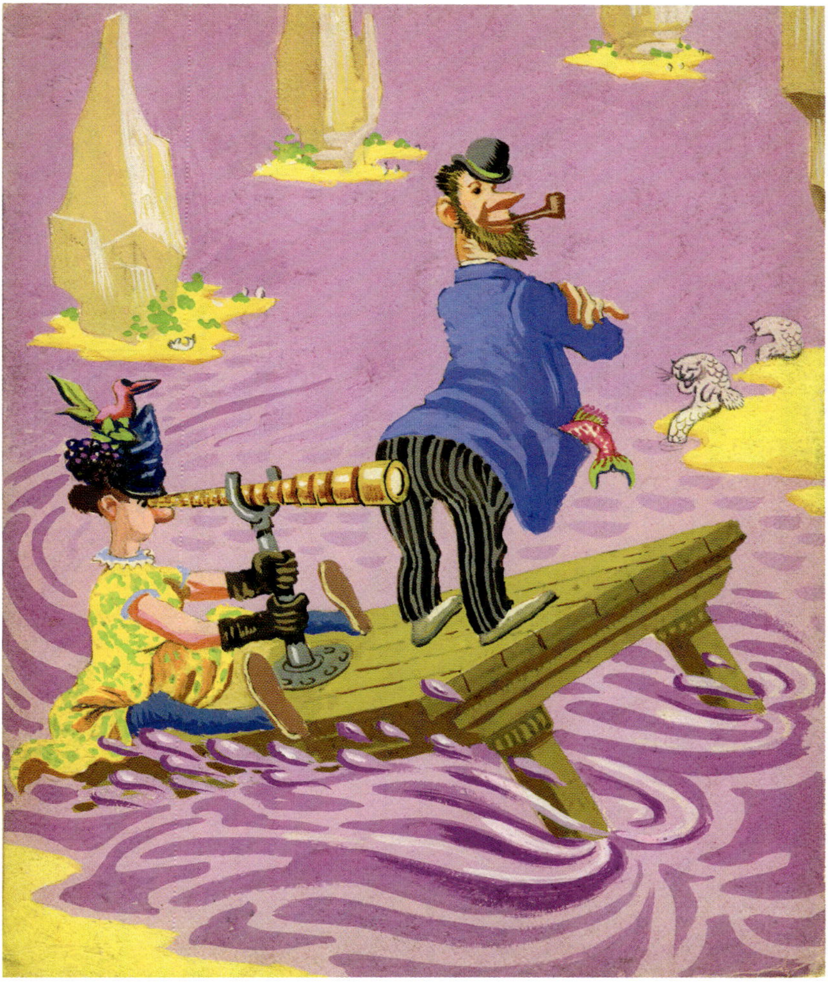

The Sunlight Falls Upon the Grass

The sunlight falls upon the grass;
    It falls upon the tower;
Upon my spectacles of brass
    It falls with all its power.

It falls on everything it can,
    For that is how it's made;
And it would fall on me, except,
    That I am in the shade.

(1944)

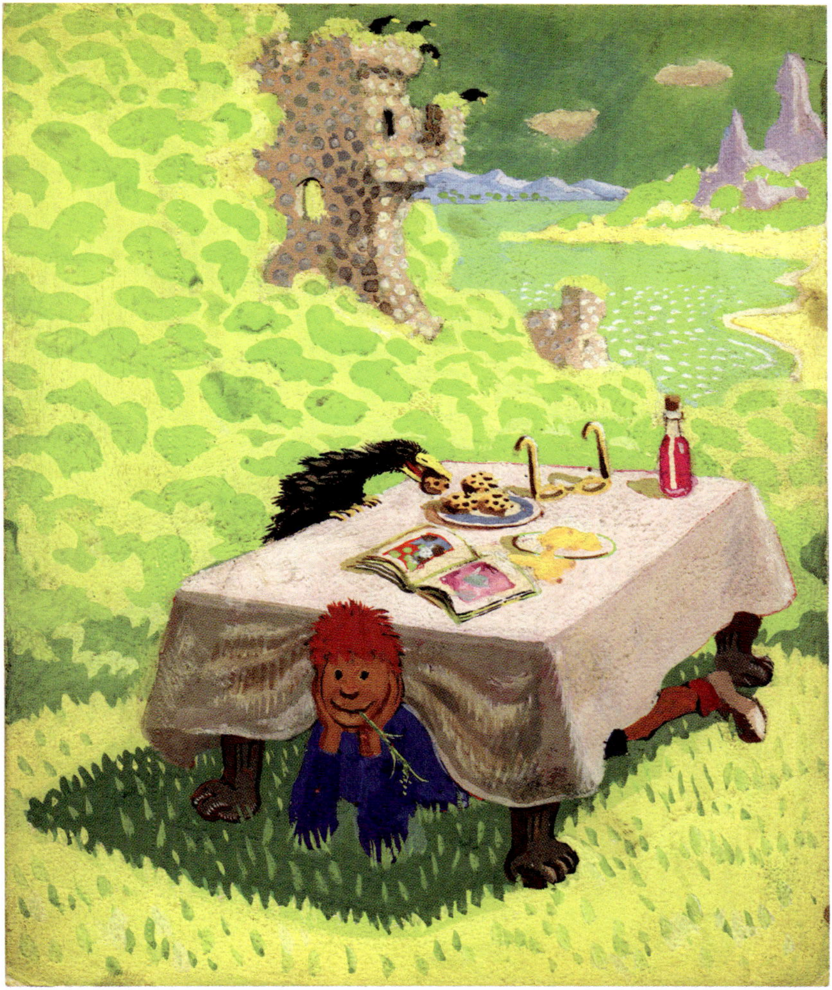

The Crocodile

A Crocodile in ecstasy
Sat on the sofa next to me
As I poured out the Indian tea.

I stared at him with startled eyes,
And wondered at his bird-like cries –
Such *little* sounds, from *such* a size.

(1944)

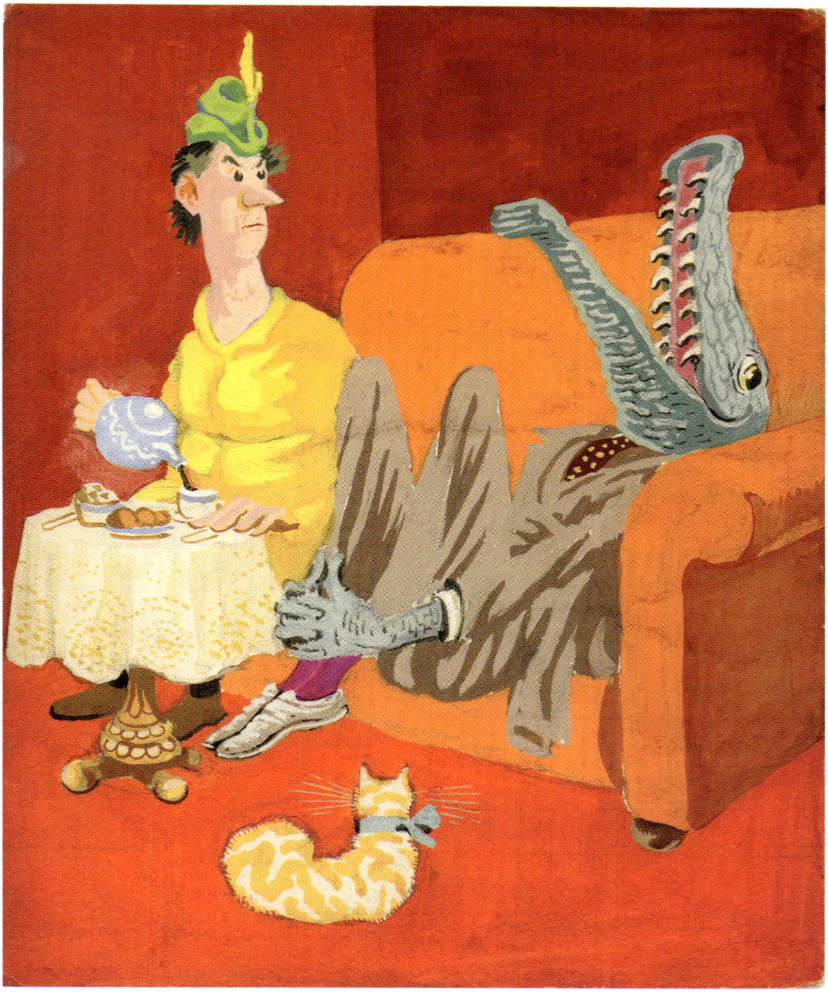

The Giraffe

You may think that he's rather slow
    At seeing jokes, but O, dear no,
It isn't that at all, and I
    Will furnish you the reason why.

You see, with such a Normus Neck,
    It takes his laughter half a week
To climb so very far from where
    It started from, which isn't fair –

Because, when it has reached his face,
    He finds that he has *lost the place*,
And can't remember what was so
    Amusing half a week ago!

(1944)

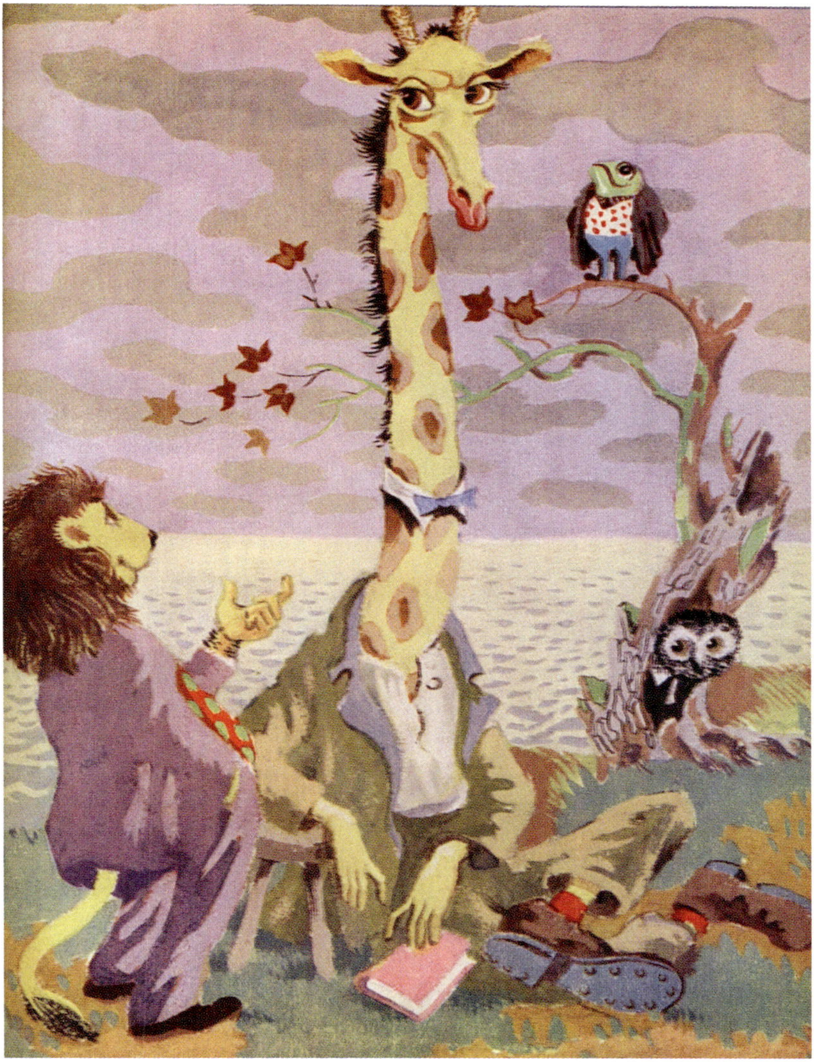

My Uncle Paul of Pimlico

My Uncle Paul of Pimlico
Has seven cats as white as snow,
Who sit at his enormous feet
And watch him, as a special treat,
Play the piano upside-down,
In his delightful dressing-gown;
The firelight leaps, the parlour glows,
And, while the music ebbs and flows,
They smile (while purring the refrains),
At little thoughts that cross their brains.

(1944)

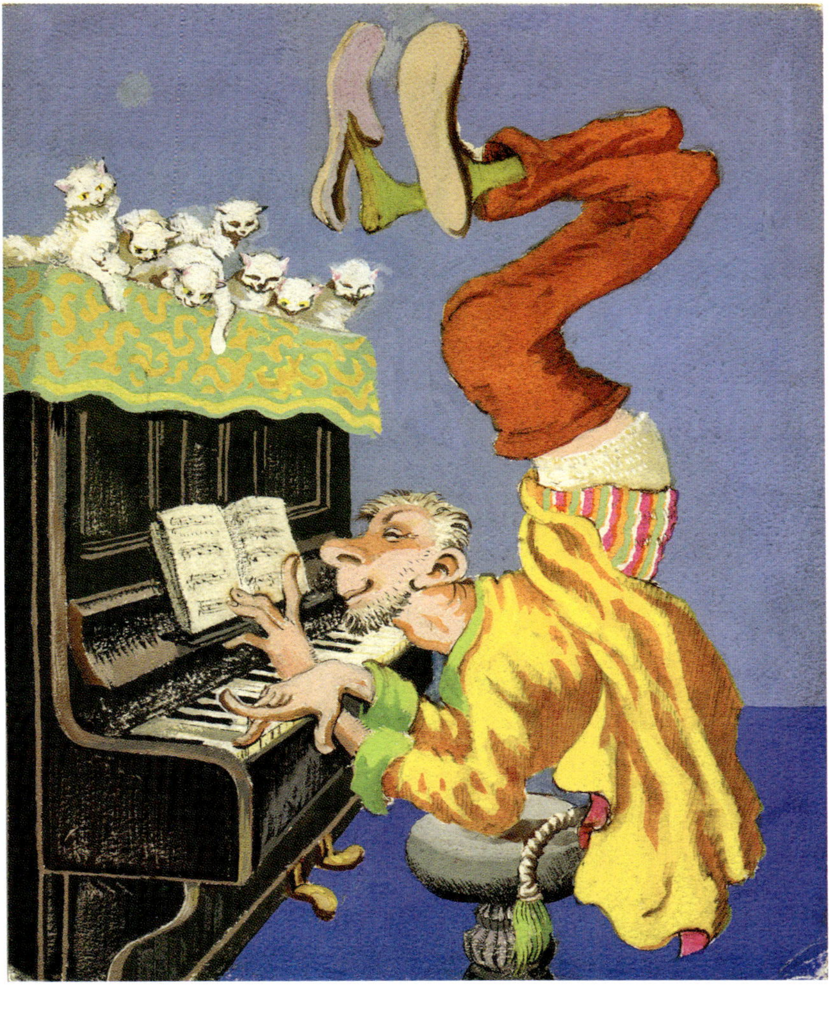

It Makes a Change

There's nothing makes a Greenland Whale
    Feel half so high-and-mighty,
As sitting on a mantelpiece
    In Aunty Mabel's nighty.

It makes a change from Freezing Seas,
    (Of which a Whale can tire),
To warm his weary tail at ease
    Before an English fire.

For this delight he leaves the sea,
    (Unknown to Aunty Mabel),
Returning only when the dawn
    Lights up the Breakfast Table.

(1944)

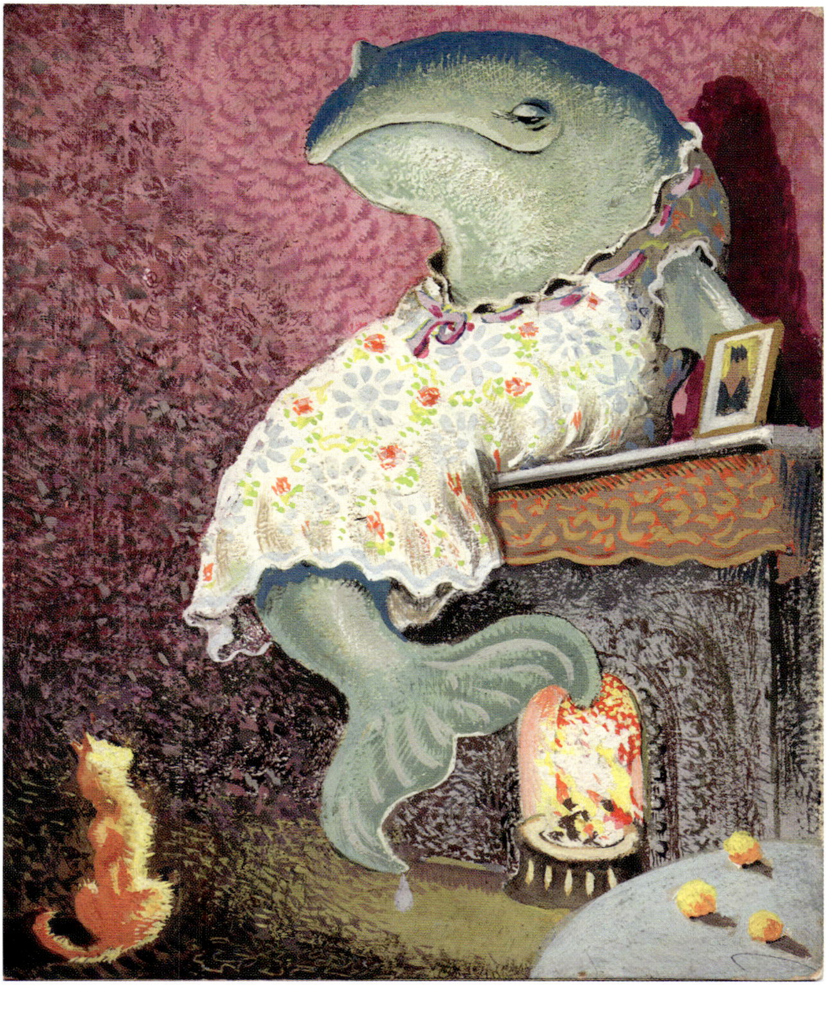

What a Day It's Been!

Dear children, what a day it's been!
    The kind of day when days
Are not what they are meant to be
    In several kind of ways.

My eyes are dim for I have sobbed
    Twelve tears of Platform Brine,
There'll *never* be another Niece
    As innocent as mine!

Mine was the One! Mine was the Two;
    Mine was the Three and Four,
And I have heard her parents say,
    She rose to Seven or more!

So be it. She is gone, and I
    Am left at Waterloo;
Half magical, half tragical,
    And, half-an-hour… or two.

(1944)

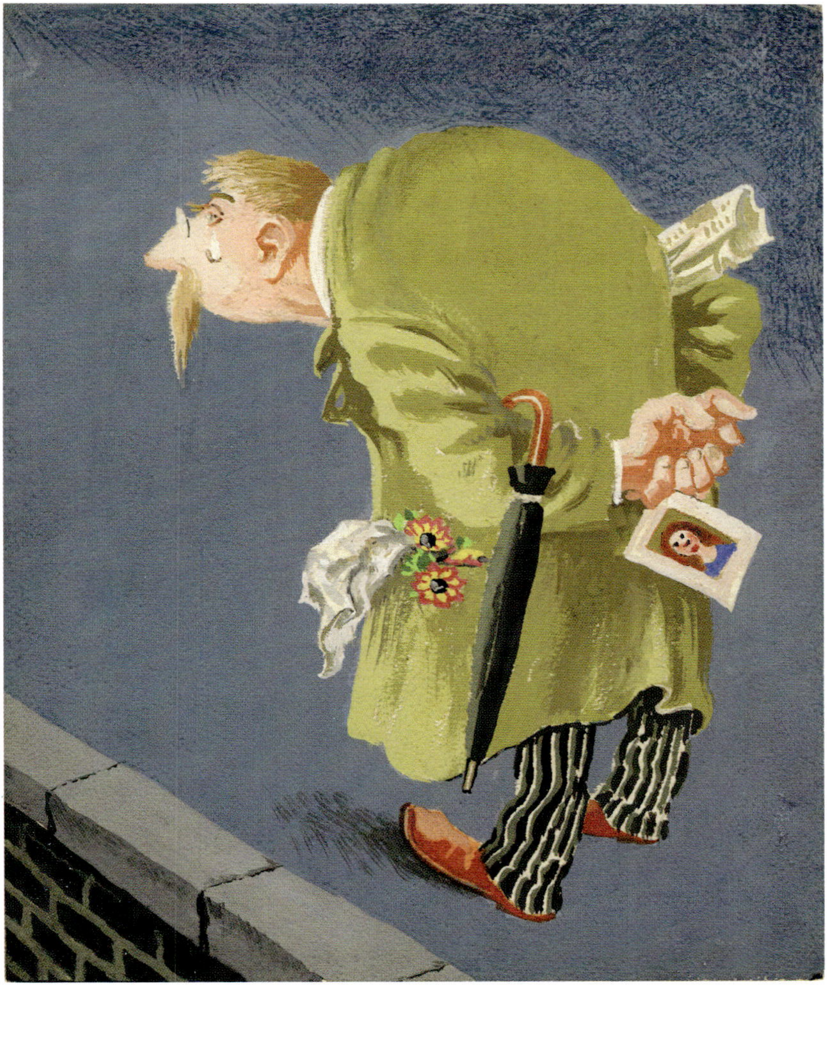

How Mournful to Imagine

Our Ears, you know, have Other Uses,
    For, when we are dead,
The Coloured Pirates swarm ashore
    And chop them off one's head!

Far out at sea, beneath the stars
    They sew them into Sails,
So that their wicked ships can leap
    Among the Killer whales.

How *mournful* to imagine
    Our poor Ears being furled
By pirates in some purple bay
    Half-way across the world!

(1944)

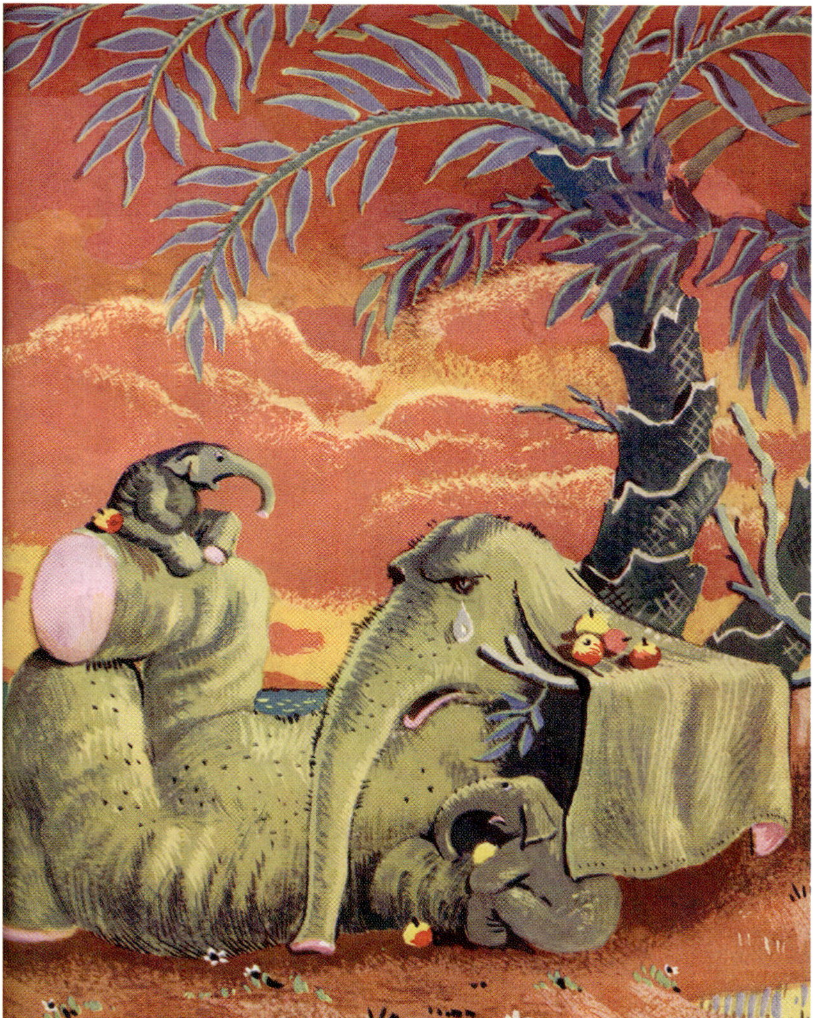

The Jailor and the Jaguar

The Jailor and the Jaguar
    Keep wandering through the rain,
The Jailor with a Swaguar,
    The Jaguar with a Pain.

They search for Warmth and Clothes to Mend,
    But mostly for their Wives,
Who left them long ago to lend
    More Colour to their Lives.

(1944)

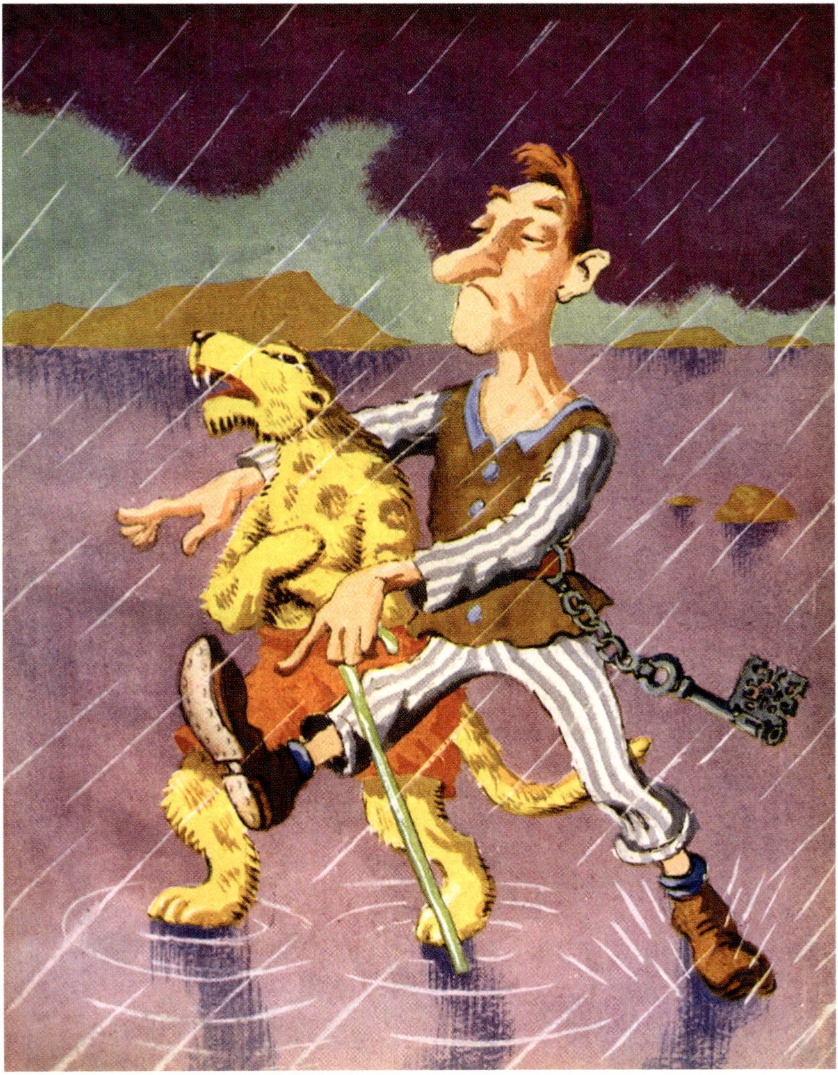

The Camel

I saw a camel sit astride
    A rainbow in the spring;
His arms were crossed, his yellow hide
    Was of the finest string.

The rainbow light upon his twine
    Had set it all aglow
With love and tinctures as divine
    As one could wish to know.

He edged along the slender arc,
    And then he rolled his eyes.
Below him the sepulchral dark
    Surged past his hairy thighs…

And then, he *sang!* but as his voice
    Was very far removed,
I first mistook it for the noise
    Of those whom once I loved.

(1944)

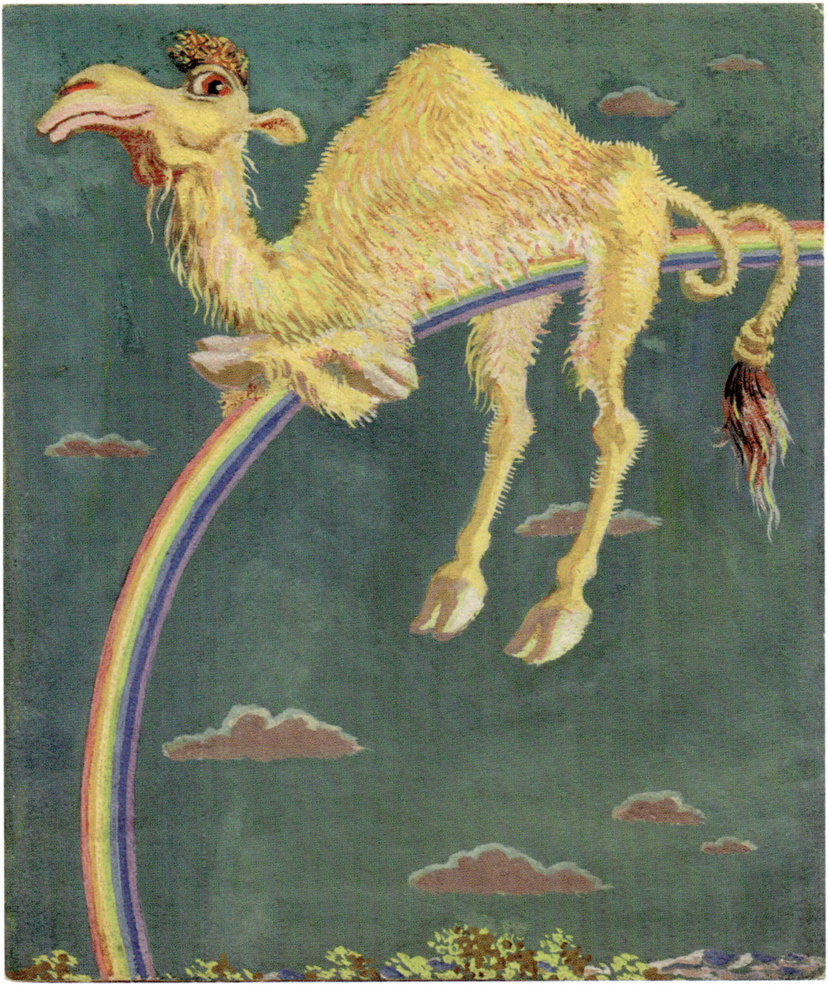

I Wish I Could Remember

Along my weary whiskers
    The tears flow fast and free,
They twinkle in the Arctic
    And plop into the sea.

Alas! my weary whiskers!
    Alas! my tearfulness!
I *wish* I could remember
    The *cause* of my distress.

(1944)

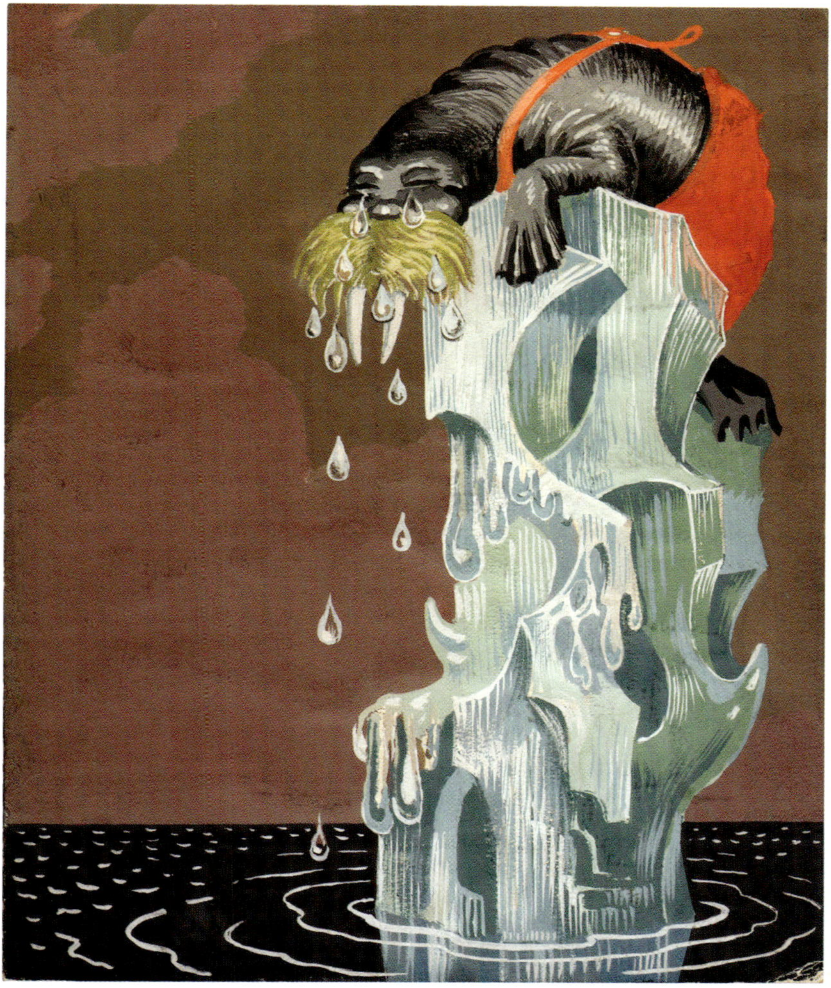

I Waxes and I Wanes, Sir

I waxes, and I wanes, sir;
    I ebbs's and I flows;
Some says it be my Brains, sir,
    Some says it be my Nose.

It isn't as I'm slow, sir,
    (To cut a story long),
It's just I'd *love* to know, sir,
    Which one of them is *wrong*.

(1944)

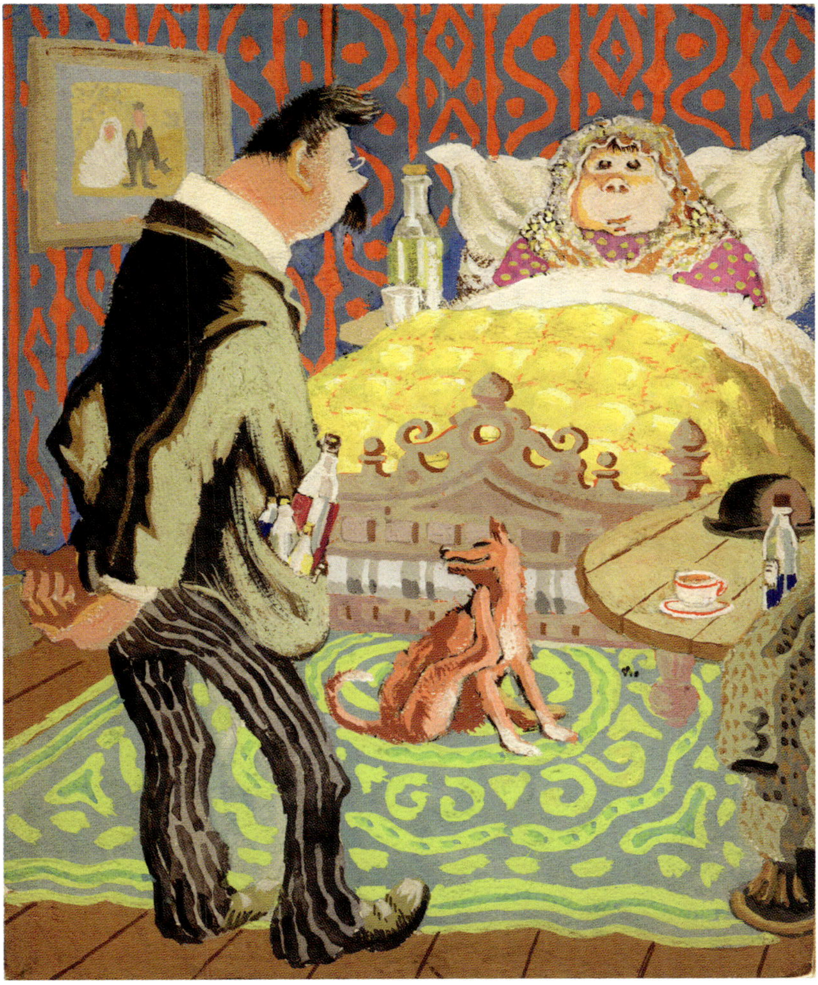

The Hippopotamus

The very nastiest grimace
    You make upon the sly,
Is *choice* beside the Hippo's face
    Who doesn't even try.

(1944)

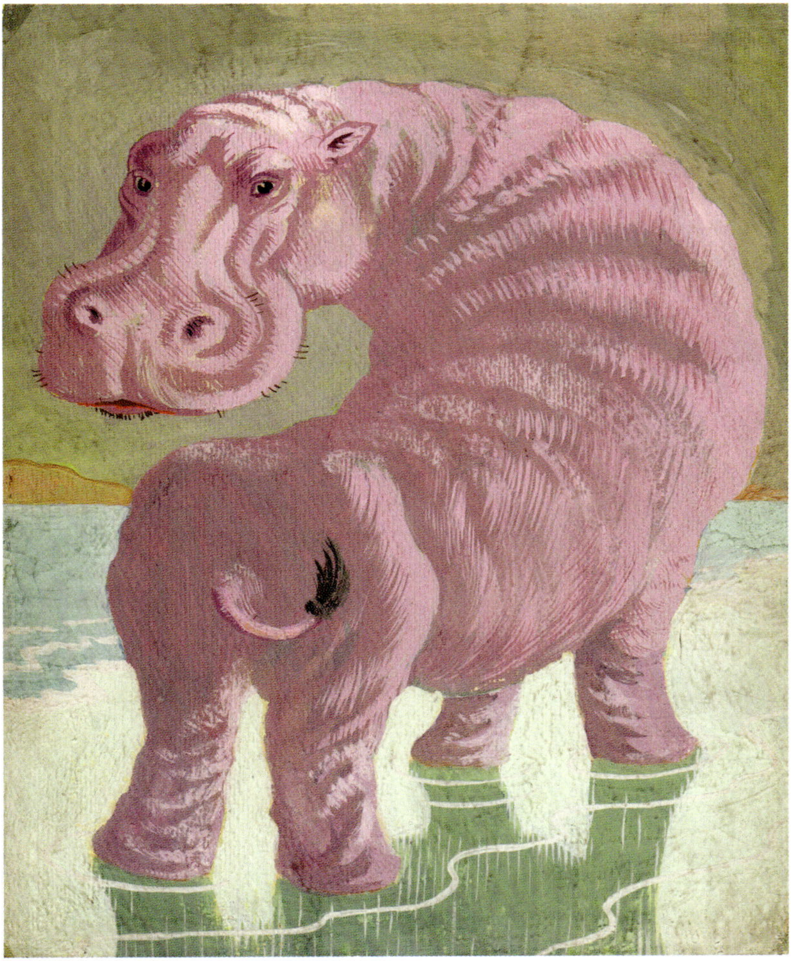

A Languorous Life

A languorous life I lead, I do
    Lead *such* a languorous life.
I lead it Here, I lead it There,
    Together with my wife.

Sometimes we lead it Round-and-round,
    And sometimes Through-and-through;
It is a life we recommend
    To anyone like You.

(1944)

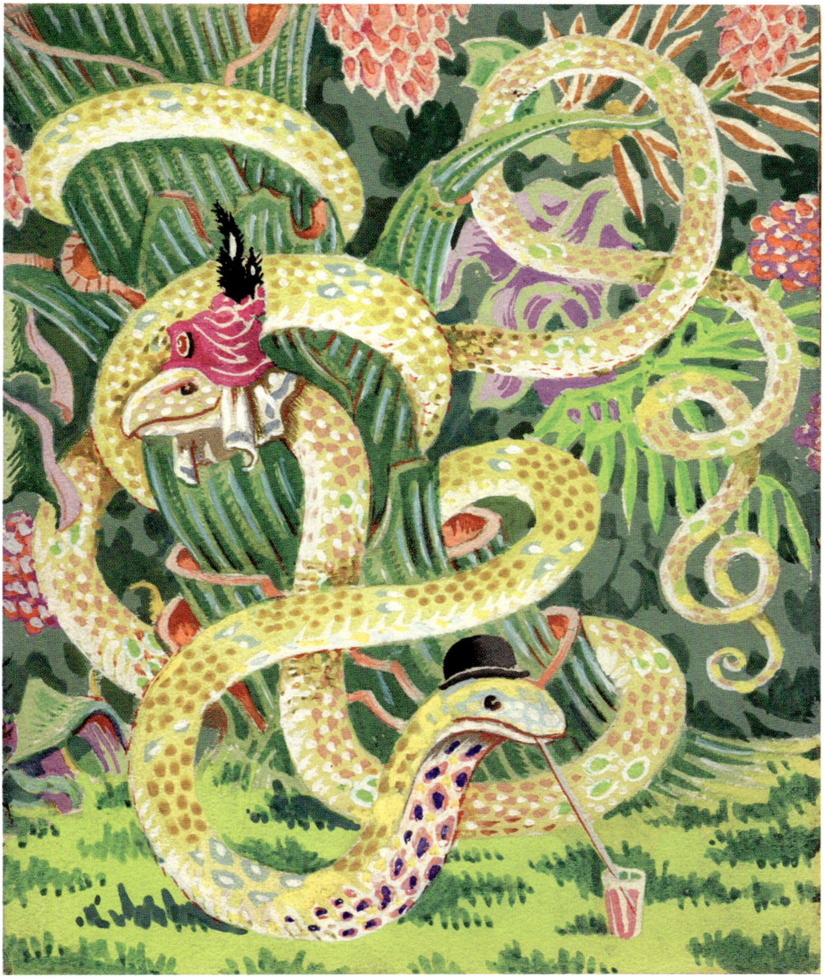

Sensitive, Seldom and Sad

Sensitive, Seldom and Sad are we,
As we wend our way to the sneezing sea,
With our hampers full of thistles and fronds
To plant round the edge of the dab-fish ponds;
O, so Sensitive, Seldom and Sad –
Oh, *so* Seldom and Sad.

In the shambling shades of the shelving shore,
We will sing us a song of the Long Before,
And light a red fire and warm our paws
For it's chilly, it is, on the Desolate shores,
For those who are Sensitive, Seldom and Sad,
For those who are Seldom and Sad.

Sensitive, Seldom and Sad we are,
As we wander along through Lands Afar,
To the sneezing sea, where the sea-weeds be,
And the dab-fish ponds that are waiting for we
Who are, Oh, so Sensitive, Seldom and Sad,
Oh *so* Seldom and Sad.

(1944)

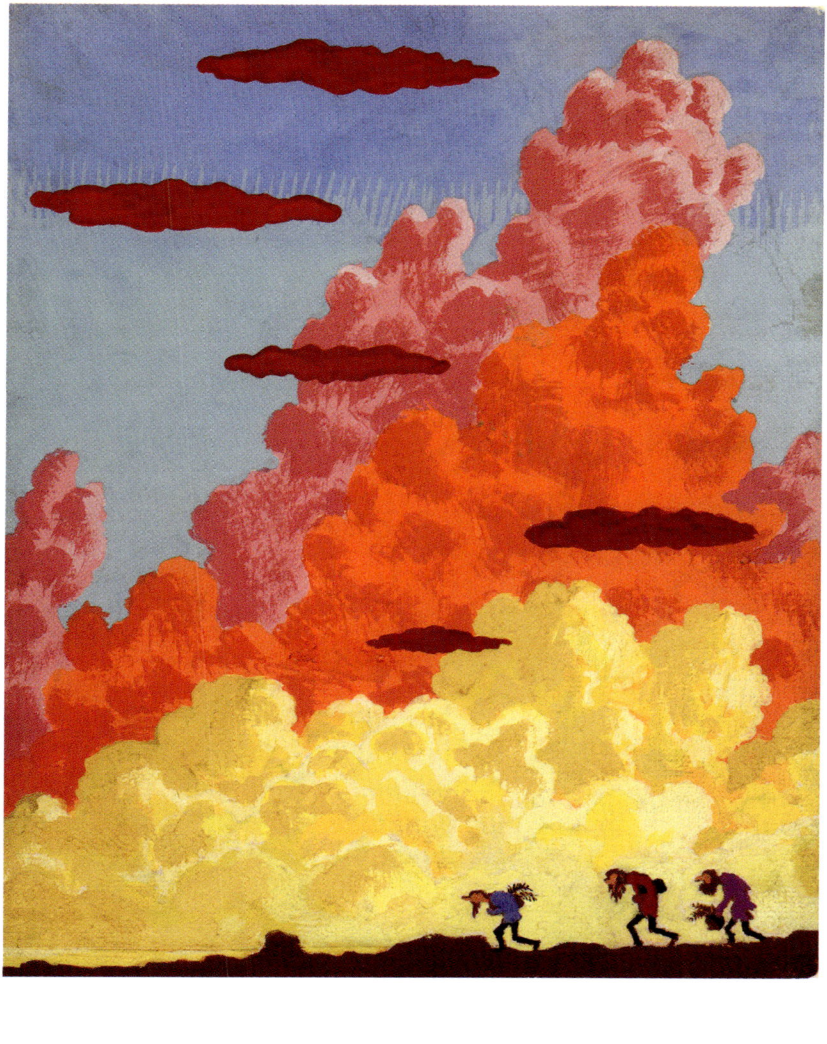

Roll Them Down

Roll them down
And down
And roll them
Down
Through the vales
Of the skulls
Where the
Winds
Bring the hails
To the valleys
Where the bulls
Roar hell
Through the alleys
Of the hills
Of rock
Stock-still
As the lock-
Jaw bones
That groan
To the tri-
Coloured sky
And the lean
White colt
As halts
By the vaults
Of the green
Thunderbolts
Is seen
Quite plain
With stars
And little fishes
In his
Mane.

(c. 1946)

One Day When They Had Settled Down

Deliria was seven foot five
And Jones was five foot seven
Deliria she gobbled fruit,
And Jones – he dreamed of heaven.
In great thick dusty books he read
And hardly ever went to bed
Before it was eleven.

One day when they had settled down
To face the other way,
A yellow lion in his prime
Crept through the mountains grey,
And – smiling like a buttercup,
Pulled off his socks and ate them up –
There is no more to say.

(1946)

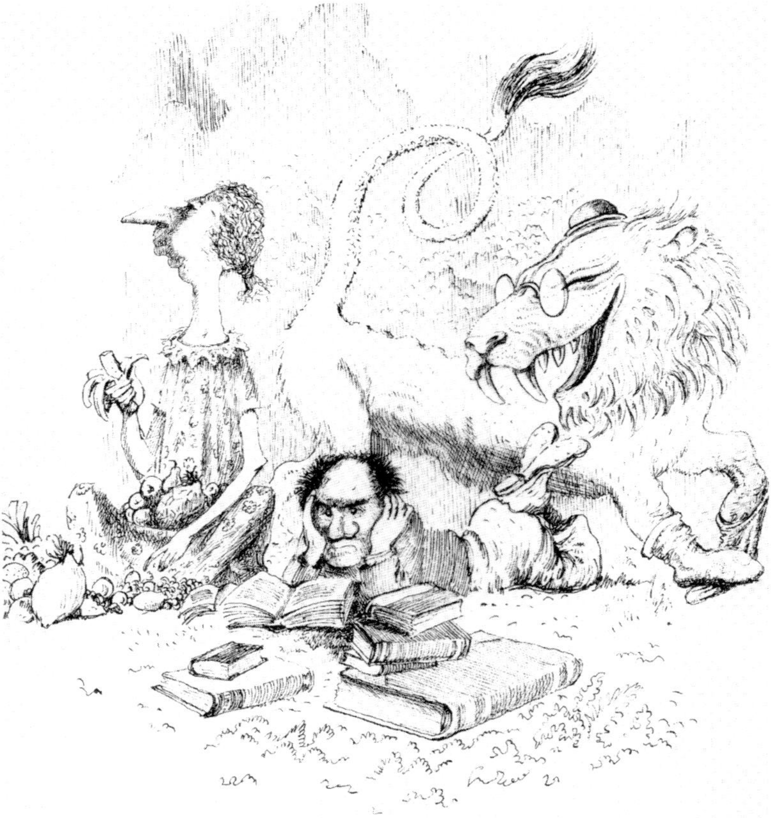

Again! Again! and Yet Again

Again! again! and yet again
I find my skull's too small
For all the jokes that throng my Brain
And have no point at all!

(1946)

Uncle George

Uncle George became so nosey
That we bought him a tea-cosy

To defend ourselves, and bring
Confusion to the evil Thing;

Which angered him so much, we had
To tie him to a blotting pad

Which soaks his energy away
From dawn to dusk, and dusk to day,

Until he's now so out of joint
That he can never see the point.

(1946)

The King of Ranga-Tanga-Roon

The King of Ranga-Tanga-Roon
Ate catfish with a golden spoon

And growled beneath the steaming sun
Until his wife was ninety-one.

The bright blue waters danced about
His island till the fish came out

And sang 'O Ranga-Tanga-Roo,
Your wife will soon be ninety-two!'

(1946)

I Cannot Give You Reasons

I cannot give you reasons
But I can give you Facts
About the way that grocers plunge
Through bubbling cataracts.

I saw them in the moonlight
A hundred miles from home –
Their pockets full of goldfish,
Their trousers full of foam.

What is the use of hiding
The secret any more?
I saw them, though I'm glad to say,
They didn't see I saw.

(1946)

The Ballad of Sweet Pighead

1

Sweet Pighead, youngest of the family,
Loved with a secret, scared embarrassment
By her startled mother, throve, and grew to be
The toast of a divided continent.

2

Her father, when he saw her in her cot,
Recovered slowly and then hanged himself.
Her only sister, rooted to the spot,
Tore off her clothes and swore she was an elf –

3

By contrast she was human but no elf
So to the black asylum she was taken –
Of this sweet Pighead knew no more than Ralph
Her uncle, long since dead, whom none can waken.

4

Her brothers saw in her, this new born child,
A family disgrace, something indecent.
One hid himself in Greece, where he reviled
The Saxon race – another, northward bent,

5

Brooded in igloos, or to staunch this wound
To everything his soul believed in, swam
From floe to floe, or with peculiar bounds
Pursued the Arctic sun as red as jam.

6

The third burned incense in the dark of night
To shrive himself of such a carnal sister.
By day he was a draper, with his white
Impassive face of razor cuts and plaster.

7

He left the red brick house where he'd been born
With all its thirty well appointed rooms
And took a flat in Palmer's Green alone
Beside a brand new graveyard of bright tombs.

8

And so the family, reduced to two,
Lived on in Fairmould Square, the frightened mother
Eyeing her little child who gently grew
From hour to hour like roses in mild weather.

9

The mother dropped her friends, she locked her doors,
Dismissed her servants – drew her curtains close,
Appalled and puzzled, but without a pause
In her maternal succour, tended her rose.

10

She was a perfect child, dressed in her long
White silken nightdress – how could anyone
But say that she was perfect as a song
Of delphic rapture lifting to the moon?

11

Sweet Pighead grew – still hidden from men's sight:
Her little snout, her delicate, dawn-lit ears,
Her alabaster skin that lapped the light,
Her tiny eyes, her amber coloured tears.

12

Her nursery was spacious, and the air
Balmy, that through the open skylight swam.
The walls were ducks-egg blue, the furniture
Was lemon yellow, with a hint of cream.

From *Figures of Speech*. The Key to the drawing is on p. 234.

13

It was not long before her mother saw
Her porcine babe with less of fear than pride.
At six weeks old she'd learned to semaphore,
And took the seven times table in her stride.

14

At eighteen months, with Euclid at her back,
And Plato in the pocket of her nighty,
Her mother realized the gulphous lack
Of her own brain in face of this almighty

15

Proffering that lay there in the cot,
A charming smile upon its delicate lips,
The gentle wrinkling of the satin snout,
The wise eyes toying with apocalypse.

16

Her mother, gushing with a naked pride,
Doted upon the brilliant freak she bore,
Yet awed by this uncalculable tide
Of sentience, was terrified the more.

17

One day, in Pighead's second year, the child
Spoke quietly, 'Come, come, you're overwrought,
Let us go out, the air is soft and mild.
I'd like to see the world I've read about.'

18

Her mother wrung her hands, and knelt beside
The infant sitting cross legged on the floor.
'Dear mother,' said Sweet Pighead, 'do not hide
Your thoughts from me, because they show the more.

19

'Of my uniqueness I'm aware, and that
Though I'm conventionally formed elsewhere
My poor head is a pig's.' She touched her snout
And lifted up the tips of either ear.

20

'I've given deep and serious thought, dear mother,
And know how I shall probably affect
And shock the populace – why bother
To palliate their lack of intellect?

21

'I have considered how I shall be shunned
And how I shall be gaped upon, and how
The answer to the problem, I have found,
Demands unflinching courage, blow for blow…'

(10 March 1947)

Hold Fast

Hold fast
To the law
Of the last
Cold tome,
Where the earth
Of the truth
Lies thick
On the page,
And the loam
Of faith
In the ink
Long fled
From the drone
Of the nib

Flows on
Through the breath
Of the bone
Reborn
In a dawn
Of doom
Where blooms
The rose
For the winds
The Child
For the tomb
The thrush
For the hush
Of song,
The corn
For the scythe
And the thorn
In wait
For the heart
Till the last
Of the first
Depart,
And the least
Of the past
Is dust
And the dust
Is lost.
Hold fast!

(c. 1947)

I Must Begin to Comprehend

I must begin to comprehend
My loves, because of my
Disorganised desire to live
Before it's time to die.

First there's the love I bear my friends,
(A poor and sickly thing.)
And secondly my love for George –
I keep him on a string.

And then there's all the love I store
And lavish on myself;
A healthy and a freckled beast
(I keep it on a shelf.)

So now I know myself and I
Can start my life anew.
Half tragical, half magical,
And half an hour, or two.

(c. 1947)

The Threads Remain

The threads remain, and cotton ones
Last longer than a thought
Which takes so long before it's sold,
And dies before it's bought.

I must begin to classify
My loves, because of my
Disorganised desire to live
Before it's time to die.

First there's the love I bear my friends,
(A poor and sickly thing)
And then my love for all that long
Wild family of String.

Such as the brothers Chord and Twine
And Uncle Rope, who's bred
With cotton on the brain, and all
My love is based on thread.

Then there is all the love I store
And lavish on myself
A healthy and a freckled beast
(I keep it on a shelf)

So now I know myself and I
Can start my life anew
Half magical, half tragical
And half-an-hour, or two.

(c. 1947)

White Mules at Prayer

White mules at prayer! Ignore them. Turn to me
Until the gold contraption of our love
Rattles its seven bright boxes and the sea
Withdraws its breakers from the Rhubarb Grove.

Combe out your zephyrs from the comely heads
Of combers, with your complex combes, the hair
Of their commotion! For the pillowy beds
Are made to float like Ida, down the air.

Why not! with feathers for their cargo, yea
And sheets at large to be so closely hauled
That one might think no blanket of the spray
But waits its bolster from another world.

This is no place where maudlin-headed fays
Can smirk behind their mushrooms: 'tis a shore
For gaping daemons. It is such a place
As I, my love, have long been looking for.

Here where the rhubarb grove into the wave
Throws down its rueful image, we can fly
Our kites of love above the sandy grave
Of those long drowned in love's dubiety.

For love is ripest by a rhubarb grove
When weird reflections glimmer through the dawn.
O Iridescence vegetably wove
Of hues that die the moment they are born.

O love, lob-sided love! how long ago
My antler'd antics pranced through halls of dread.
The Alps of God stood silent in a row
A dunce's cap of snow on every head.

Chill was the air, chill on the brow, & very
Close for all that, because the day was warm.
The screaming gale gave little presage, really,
Or sign of any *future* kind of storm.

Lost in the venal world our dreams deflate
By easy stages through green atmosphere.
Imagination's taut balloon is late
In coming up, like the blue whale, for air.

It is not known what genus of the wild
Blue plums of thought best wrinkle, twitch and flow
Into black wisdom's prune, for in the mild
Orchards of love there is no need to know.

No need at all, for us to wander back
Into the core of what one day might be
The kind of nut no argument can crack –
What is it, friend, that stirs the Indian tea?

No! not the hollow heron-crested prince
Of porcelain spurs the white steeds of the south,
Rather, some ragged mendicant shall prance
With wisdom like an acorn in his mouth.

What use to cry for Capricorn? it sails
Across the heart's red atlas; it is found
Only within the skull, where all the tails
The tempest has are whisking it around.

No time for tears! It is enough today
That we, meandering these granular shores,
Can watch the ponderous billows at their play
Like midnight beasts with garlands in their jaws.

But hush! Along the winds the turkey-breasted
Clouds involve our spirit with their flight.
Cover the eyes; you *can't* be interested.
Bandage your eyes with seaweed for tonight.

White mules at prayer! I wish they'd go away
Or else you would not stare at them so deep.
The sea-gloom thickens. Hark! within the spray
I hear the mermaids munching in their sleep.

(c. 1947)

O Love, O Death, O Ecstasy

1

O love, O death, O ecstasy
Beneath the moon's marmoreal snout!
O rhubarb burning by the sea
Through nights of nought and days of doubt
Ah pity me, Ah pity me,
What is it all about?
What is it all about?

2

A voice across the coughing brine
Has sewn your spirit into mine!
O love it is for me to die
Upon your bosom noisily,
Ah pity me, ah pity me,
What is it all about?
What is it all about?

(c. 1947)

Tintinnabulum

1

There was a man came up to me,
He said, 'I know you well:
Within your face I'm sure I see
The tinkling of a bell.'

2

I said to him, 'I rather doubt
We've ever met before!
I cannot recollect your snout.
Retire, and say no more.'

3

But he continued – 'I recall
Our meeting long ago,
Your face amazed me then, with all
Its tinkles, don't you know.'

4

He put his ear within a good
Four inches of the space
On which my features sit and brood –
And listened to my face.

5

'Just so,' he said at last; 'just so.
Sit down, O tinkly one.
Here, in the cool our thoughts can flow
To where they first begun.'

From *Figures of Speech*. The Key to the drawing is on p. 234.

6

I said, 'I know you not: nor where
You live: nor who you be
And much resent the way you stare
Exclusively at me.'

7

'It is the tinkling, sir,' he said.
'Your face is pastoral.
Behind its monstrousness are spread
The meadows lush and cool.

8

'Behind the hot, ridiculous
Red face of you, there ring
The bells of youth, melodious
As sheepfolds in the spring.

9

'I'm sure I'm not mistaken, sir
My ears could not forget
A face with such interior
Melodies, dry or wet.

10

'I must have met you long ago,
In Maida Vale, I think
When the canal was bright with snow
And black with Indian ink.

11

'Beneath an archway, on a stair
(The harvest moon was full –
And ripe as any yellow pear
That tastes of cotton wool) –

12

'I saw your shape descend on me –
It all comes gaily back –
You stood and tried to bend on me
Your eyes of button-black –

13

'Away, away, I heard you cry –
(Just as you have today –
Without a wherefore or a why,
I had to disobey)

14

'Away! away! I heard you say
But swiftly I replied
I've every kind of right to stay –
The law is on my side.

15

'"No *moral right*, no *moral right*,"
You screamed, in double prose,
"You have no case at all tonight
I am the man who knows" –

16

'And then – you *tinkled!* 'Twas that sound
That cantered through my ears
And thence into a vale profound
Too deep for human tears.'

17

'No, no, no, no, it is not so!
Your memory's at fault!
How can such recollections grow
On boughs of biblic salt?

18

'It was not me, for I am not
The tinkling type,' I said.
'I am a businessman, I've got
A bowler on my head.'

19

'Mere counterfeit,' the man replied,
'That symbol of the grave
Could never even hope to hide
That *you* are not a slave.

20

'There is a sparkle in your eye,
A lightness in your tread –
And your demeanour crisp and spry
Leaves nothing to be said.

21

'Give up your soul. Deny your pride,
Confess your guilt, and be
Unutterably on my side
Before we go to tea.

22

'Though I'm a stranger, can't you feel
Our kinship – otherwise
How could your presence, soft as veal
Bring tears into my eyes?

23

'Turn over a fresh page my friend
And turn it over fast –
For no one knows how soon may end
The foolscap of your past.

24

'Come, let me hold you by the raw
Black elbow of your coat.
Your courage mounts; O leave the shore
While this is yet a boat.

25

'I am your boat! I am your crew
Your rudder or your mast –
Yea friend, I am your limpets too
And your elastoplast.'

26

How could I fail to be inspired
By words so hotly said.
I found my inner faith was fired,
The blood rushed to my head.

27

'O stranger, I will tell you all!
I am the man, I was
So nervous of my inner bell –
Especially out of doors.

28

'But I am he: the tinkly one.
What I can do, I will.'
Said he – 'See how the golden sun
Sits on that pea-green hill.

29

'It is a sign. You have confessed.
Your finer self breaks through –
Even the flowers your boots have pressed
Are ogling in the dew.

30

'Sit down, sit down,' he said. I squatted
On the sparkling pasture.
The rain came down and filled my spotted
Shirt with pleasant moisture.

31

A kind of ecstasy descended
With the rain on me –
And gradually I unbended
Metaphysically.

32

Sweet genesis! my tingling thumbs
Described wide arcs so bright!
They might have been those starry crumbs
That skid the arctic night.

33

And by exorbitant degrees
My body grew involved,
Until the problem of my knees
And elbows were resolved.

34

Until my brain grew clearer far
Than it had ever been
That both my ears, now kept ajar
Might hear what I had seen.

35

'If it be so, that quite unknown
To friends, I tinkle, stranger
Please tell me, am I quite alone
In this – and is there danger?'

36

He listened once again, his ear
Close to my face, and cried,
'There is no danger – yet, I hear
Such silvery sounds inside,

37

'Such sounds as fairies pluck from strings
Of starbeams, in the dew –
O Lord it is a moving thing
To listen, sir, to you.'

38

His ear was very near my face,
I bit it once, for fun.
He said, 'You ought to know your place,
With friendship newly born.'

39

'I trusted you,' I said, 'to know
The friendly way I meant it.'
'Ah well,' he said, 'I'll get to know
Your ways, and won't resent it.'

40

He listened once again. I kept
Immobile, an improvement
So great, he said my tinkling leapt
Straight through the second movement.

41

Such dulcet sounds as might inspire
A broker with the thrill
Of consummating his desire
To hug a daffodil.

42

Again I spoke, 'O tell me, am
I quite alone in this
Weird tintinnabulation, Sam –
Is it indigenous?'

43

I called him Sam, because I felt
Our friendship, strange and quick
Needed cementing. Would he melt?
And call me Roderick?

44

He did – there was no doubt a svelte
And psychic power possessed us –
For neither name was one which spelt
The proof of our asbestos.

45

'Am I alone?' I once again
Reverted to my theme,
'Do other tinklers wake the strain
Of cowbells in the cream?'

46

'There are three others who have this
Peculiar trait. They are
A grocer bred in Pontefrice
A bison and a Tsar.

47

'You are the fourth and I will prove
Your excellence to all.
Cast off that symbol of the grave
Your bowler and your pall.'

48

His arguments had been so fair
And what is more I knew
That there was really something there
That needed seeing to.

49

So, standing in the lashing rain
I wrenched my hat away
From my haematic head, in pain
And then, symbolically,

50

(His eyes were on me all the while)
I flung the symbol through
The downpour with the kind of smile
That needs attending to.

51

And I was free! and now my goal
Is on a different plane
And I will never let my soul
Be rude to me again.

(c. 1947)

Squat Ursula

1

Squat Ursula the golden
With such wild beauty blest,
That when a man's beholden
Her glory – heel to crest –
He rests – if he's an old'n
It's wise to take a rest.

2

Squat Ursula the golden
Can tire the young men too,
Because her limbs are moulden
From honey, milk and dew,
And April leaves, and olden
Magic – and Irish stew.

3

But Ursula has vanished
With some unbridled boy
Along with pictures varnished
With swamps of sepia gloy –
Along with bronzes burnished,
And all the tripe of Troy.

4

O Ursula, Squat Ursula,
Wild Ursula, recall
That night I sang a versula
Beneath the midnight wall –
And how you were so terse-ula
And sharp with me, 'n' all.

5

But you are gone; your goldness
Your wildness and your squat
Magnetic form, your coldness
That left me piping hot –
And you are gone, my olden
Flame whom I never caught!

6

Along with Saul and Moses
Along with all the lot
Who had fantastic noses
And didn't care a jot –
O Ursula! what roses
I ever plucked, or bought

7

Have been for you, my passion,
My queen of fire and dread;
Divine amalgamation
Of swedes and copper-thread,
Unstitch your irritation
And kiss me when I'm dead.

(c. 1947)

The Hideous Root

1

A Plumber appeared by the Light of the Moon
And sang like the grinding of brakes
To his wife, who made answer, which, though out of tune
And aesthetically full of mistakes
Was sweet in his ear, for he knew that it meant
She was waiting for him in their Wickerwork Tent.

2

The plumber, ignoring the Light of the Moon
Permitted his Body to Spring
Like a leaf in the wind, like a heifer in June,
Like a fish, or a bun on a string –
There was Joy in his Heart, and the Prawns in his Hair
Felt the wind in their scales as he leapt through the Air.

3

The Leap of a Plumber in tropical climes
Is a sight calculated to pluck
At the heartstrings of those who, ahead of their times
Know Skill, when they see it, from Luck –
O full of professional Zest is the sight
Of a Plumber spreadeagled in amorous flight.

4

When the Plumber had landed, his Echoes had died
Through the forest, and he was alone
With his Shadow, his Passion, his Prawns and his Pride
And his suitcase from Marylebone.
Above him the trees with their heliotrope Fruit
Reflected their sheen on his Tropical Suit.

5

His Tropical Suit, that he made long ago
In his bachelor days, 'neath a Tree,
With his Needle and Cotton a-glint in the glow
Of a sunset that sat on the sea –
The Suit that enriched seven months of his life
In the making thereof for the Eye of a Wife.

6

And a Wife soon enough had arrived on the Scene,
She had watched him, one evening of Thrills,
His Suit in the starlight was purple and green
And was garnished with Tassels and Frills.
On his shimmering sleeves there were crescents and moons
And his chest was embroidered with knives, forks and spoons.

7

His collar was seaweed dragged out of the Sea
All golden and shiny and wet.
His hat was an Elephant's Ear, that could be
Twisted up like a fresh serviette
That is perched on the Table when very clean guests
Are invited to dinner with studs in their vests.

8

Now that very same evening (the evening she saw
Him appear in his Tropical Suit)
She had stood silhouetted against the White Shore,
In her hand was the Hideous Root –
The Root, but for which he might never have known
Any Thing could be *worse* than the Face of his Own.

9

But O, it *was* worse, it was worse than a dream
Of a gargoyle coiled up in a fight
With itself, whom it bites, and decides that each scream
Is not its, but some foe's in the Night,
Far worse was this Hideous Root, that she carried
At the side of her face, even now she was married.

10

And O, to the Plumber, as lovely she is
As a rose on the brow of a fawn.
Or a dewdrop that gurgles in aqueous bliss
In tremulous light of the dawn.
How gorgeous she was, he remembered, that day
On the sands, when he wooed her and took her away.

11

'But the Root,' he had murmured, 'the Root, my most sweet!
Must it *share* in our marital life?'
She had smirked like a fairy, and wriggled her feet
Then replied, 'You must know that a Wife
Has her secrets, my dear, and this Root is my friend –
Be patient with me, though you can't Understand.'

12

The Plumber remembered the pride he had known
In taking her into his arms
Though she still held the Root very close to the bone
Which obstructed deploy of his charms
But O there was pride in his promise to never
Refer to the Root, though she clutch it for Ever.

13

The Plumber, with memories thick in his mind
Such as these that have just been related
Went bouncing along through the Forest to find
His beloved with whom he was mated –
Their Wickerwork Tent was beneath a bright tree
Where he pictured her waiting impatient as he.

14

He entered the glade with a bounce of such joy
That the serviette hat on his head
Was blown through the air though he'd fixed it with gloy
To his ears which were lilac and red.
It stuck in a tree and a bird with thick legs
Jumped inside with a bang and laid thirty-two eggs.

15

When he came to the Wickerwork Tent he gave cry
As before (like the grinding of brakes)
And peered through the Wickerwork Door with one eye
To observe the Reaction that shakes
The frame of a loving and sensitive spouse
When the cry of a husband vibrates through the House.

16

But O! the Black Horror! the Sharp Disillusion!
The Grim, Realistical Fact!
She was there, it is true, but was Coiled in Confusion
And foiled by lack of his Tact.
She had not been prepared for his Speed, nor before
Had been caught unawares when he Peered through the Door.

17

No! Never before since that Day of all Days
When he watched her against the White Shore –
No! Never before, since the fire of his praise
Had scalded her – Never before
In his life had he ever had Reason to Doubt!
(O where was the Root she was never Without?)

18

That horrible, desperate Ghoul of a Root,
That Nightmare of Twitches and Twists,
That Riot of Wrinkles from skull-piece to foot
With its surfeit of ankles and fists,
That coiling, incurable, knobbled and scarred
Monstrosity measuring nearly a yard.

19

As he looked through the wickerwork what should he spy
But his Wife in a Whirlpool of Speed –
When she stopped to draw breath he could see with one eye
She was very distracted indeed –
She had lost her Ridiculous Root, and he saw
That without it her Beauty was Never no more.

20

The Root which she held in the grip of her paw
As a foil to her negative charms
The Root that would heave with her every snore
As it lay through the night in her arms –
O the qualms that now racked him, the Root being gone
Made hay of his pride in a beauty now flown.

From *Figures of Speech*. The Key to the drawing is on p. 234.

21

For ah, in her terrible moments of rest
He could see she was frightful indeed –
The Terrible Root that had helped to invest
Her face with the bloom of her breed
Was missing! and she, being Glad of a Mate,
Was searching for It at a hideous rate.

22

The Plumber was mortified, hesitant, full
Of deep terror, but suddenly saw
The Root in the grass 'neath the Bright Tree and all
His confidence flowered once more –
He grasped it and cried to his lady within:
'Your Root! my beloved. Your Root's in my fin!'

23

At the sound, like a meteor that streams through a cloud
His mate had burst out of the tent.
As a Knife runs through butter, she sailed with a loud
And shattering sound as she went
Through the wickerwork wall of their dwelling, to land
By her husband who held the great Root in his hand.

24

She snatched at the Hideous Root in a wild
Unladylike manner, and squeezed
The hideous thing in her arms like a child

Beside her the Root by the   rule
Of stark relativity lowered the wood

25

O'er the eyes of the Plumber, and she was Once More
An ornament made for his praise.
The Root with its mystical powers of yore
Resolved her inelegant ways
And a vision of all that her beauty had been
Returned to enchant the connubial scene.

26

But now, double padlocked the Jubilant Wife
Of the Plumber has chained to her side
The Hideous Root which she guards with her life.
For what can more furnish a bride
With tranquillity, faith and a pride in her lot
Than a Foil of the kind that the lady has got?

27

So Love once again springing green in their breasts
Is dancing like meadows of corn.
Far from rootless it quivers with joy and invests
Their feet with the flight of a fawn.
O see! how the Plumber and she can gyrate,
His arm round the shuddering waist of his mate!

28

And from then until now the thrice halcyon days
Flow by them, the lady be-chained
With the Root at her belt while he floods her with praise
In a manner ornate and unfeigned,
And yet – at the back of his mind sometimes stirs
A dislike of That Root and that Secret of hers.

(c. 1947)

The Men in Bowler Hats Are Sweet

The Men in Bowler Hats are Sweet!
And dance through April showers,
So innocent! Oh it's a treat
To watch their tiny little feet
Leap nimbly through the arduous wheat
Among the lambs and flowers.

Many and many is the time
That I have watched them play,
A broker drenched in glimmering rime,
A banker, innocent of crime,
With lots of bears and bulls, in time
To share the holiday.

The grass is lush – the moss is plush,
The trees are hands at prayer.
The banker and the broker flush
To see a white rose in a bush,
And gasp with joy, and with a blush
They hug each bull and bear.

The Men in Bowler Hats are sweet
Beneath their bowler hats.
It's not their fault if, in the heat
Of their Transactions; I repeat,
It's not their fault if Vampires meet
And gurgle in their spats.

(c. 1947)

Aunts and Uncles

When Aunty Jane
Became a Crane
She put her leg behind her head;
And even when the clock struck ten
Refused to go to bed.

When Aunty Grace
Became a Plaice
She all but vanished sideways on;
Except her nose
And pointed toes
The rest of her was gone.

When Uncle Wog
Became a Dog
He hid himself for shame;
He sometimes hid his bone as well
And wouldn't hear the front-door bell,
Or answer to his name.

When Aunty Flo
Became a Crow
She had a bed put in a tree;
And there she lay
And read all day
Of ornithology.

When Aunty Vi
Became a Fly
Her favourite nephew
Sought her life;
How could he know
That with each blow
He bruised his Uncle's wife?

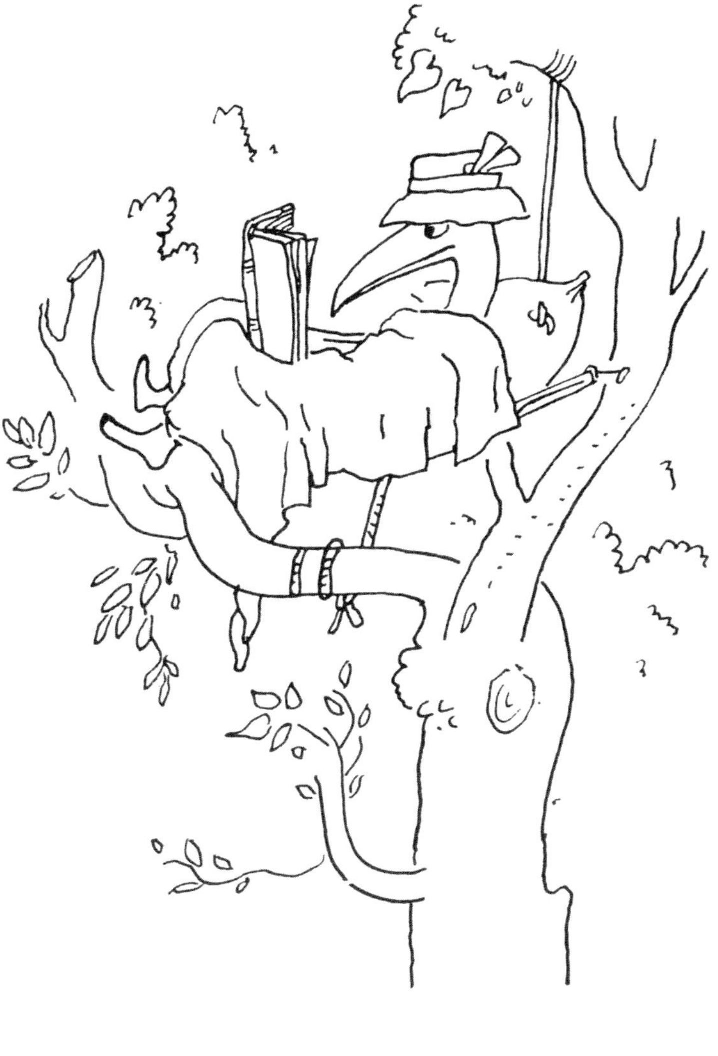

When Uncle Sam
Became a Ham
We did not care to carve him up;
He struggled so
We let him go
And gave him to the pup.

When Aunty Nag
Became a Crag
She stared across the dawn,
To where her spouse
Kept open house
With ladies on the lawn.

When Aunty Mig
Became a Pig
She floated on the briny breeze,
With irritation in her heart
And warts upon her knees.

When Aunty Jill
Became a Pill
She stared all day through dark-blue glass;
And always sneered
When men appeared
To ask her how she was.

When Uncle Jake
Became a Snake
He never found it out;
And so as no one mentions it
One sees him still about.

(c. 1947)

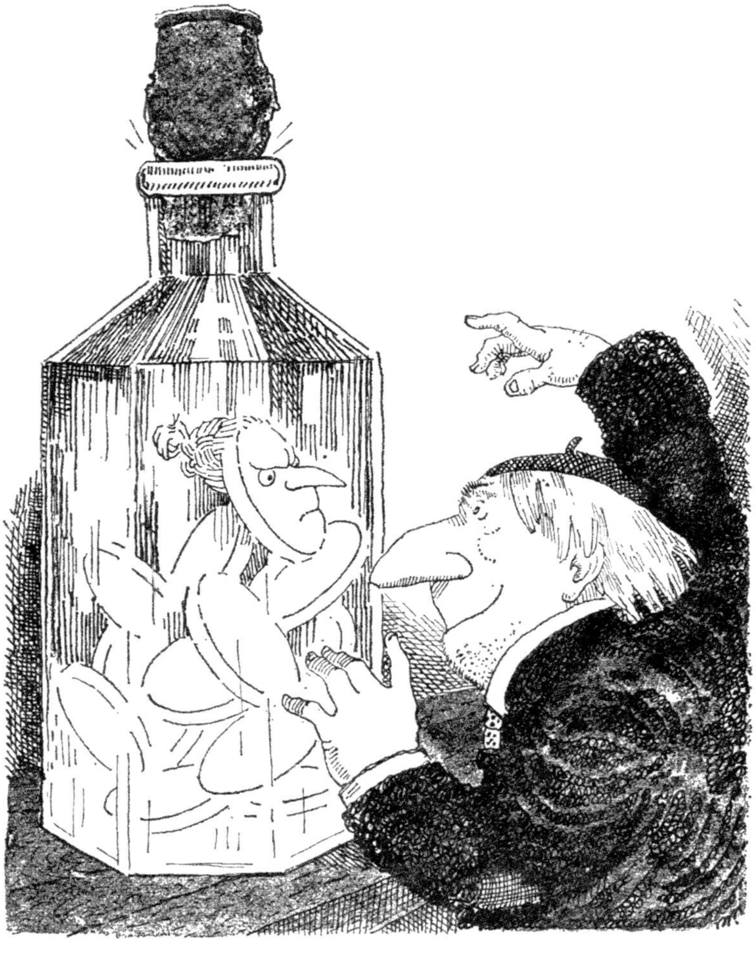

The Osseous 'Orse

Come, flick the ulna juggler-wise
      And twang the tibia for me!
O Osseous 'orse, the future lies
      Like serum on the sea.

Green fields and buttercups no more
      Regale you with delight, no, no!
The tonic tempests leap and pour
      Through your white pelvis ever so.

'Are you enjoying it, Irma?' She nodded sleepily.

Come, clap your scapulae and twitch
      The white pagoda of your spine,
Removed from life's eternal itch
      What need for iodine?

Then dine! I owe you this at least!
      Dine! in the over-rated light
Of the pig-faced moon. We'll have a feast
      To end all feasts tonight.

The Osseous 'orse sat up at once
      And clanged his ribs in biblic pride.
I fear I looked at him askance
      Though he had naught to hide…

No hide at all… just…

At this point the doctor, having forgotten what came next, turned his eyes once more to his sister Irma; she was fast asleep.

(February 1948)

From *Figures of Speech*. The Key to the drawing is on p. 234.

Song of the Castle Poet

(*To be declaimed with one foot in the air!*)

So is it always when the hairfaced hedgerow
Whores with the sucking legions and the hips
Of autumn prick and parry at the bluebud.
So was it always: down the lean perspectives
Sparkle the flecks of sunbeams, motes and needles,
(Where is the wiseman with an eye to spare?)
And over all the emerald nods and bows.

There is no never no more nor ever again
For gotten coin, or love the able semen –
See! the red timepiece on a damsel's cage
Ticks to the doomsday crack. Nor wheel nor rack
Can turn or break the brain – O island bitten
With bays that burn the brains of boys away
No laurels cast their shade across the brine
No waders dare the knee-deep estuary.

The biscuit-ship lies breathing in the bay
And every weevil cries 'aloft! aloft!'
Dry as a dove-cot in the summer evil
Love-bound and helpless in a loft of homers
How was it when we were not – how indeed?
The seasons press the age of apples homeward
And every wrinkle whets the scythe of time
Ah! make me lucid lady! make me…

Do your own dirty work muttered the Countess of Groan.

(April–May 1949)

How White and Scarlet Is that Face

How white and scarlet is that face!
Who knows, in some unusual place
The coloured heroes are alight
With faces made of red and white.

(June 1949)

O Here It Is and There It Is…

O here it is! and there it is!
And no-one knows whose share it is!
Nor dares to stake a claim –
But we have seen it in the air,
A fairy, like a William pear –
With but itself to blame.

A thug it is! and smug it is;
And like a floating pug it is,
Above the orchard trees.
It has no right – no right at all
To soar above the orchard wall,
With chilblains on its knees.

(1949)

O HERE IT IS AND THERE IT IS...

Mervyn Peake.

O here it is! and there it is!
And no-one knows whose share it is!
Nor dares to stake a claim —
But we have seen it in the air,
A fairy, like a William pear —
With but itself to blame.

A thug it is! and smug it is;
And like a floating pug it is,
Above the orchard trees.
It has no right — no right at all
To soar above the orchard wall,
With chilblains on its knees.

Have a Pear

Little Spider

Little spider
Spide-ing sadly
In the webly
Light of leaves!
What's inside a
Spide's mentadly
Makes its hebly
Full of grieves?

Little spider
Legged and lonely
In the bonely
Way of thieves
Where's the fly-da
On the phone-ly?

(1949)

'It Worries Me to Know'

'It worries me to know,' she cried,
Her voice both sharp and high:
Her dress was yellow as the hide
Of lions in July –
'It worries me to know…' she cried,
And then she rolled her eyes aside.

Her friend (a cloudy-looking man)
Began to tap his shoe.
His collar was of astrakhan,
His hair and beard was too.
'What *is* it worries you to know?'
He said in accents lush and low.

But she had rolled her eyes aside
As though she were not able
To quell an inward rise of tide
And feared to slip her cable –
He turned to where her eyes were bent
Upon a golden ornament.

'Talk not of Fancy, friend, to me,
Though you are old and wise.
My trouble is with what I see,
That's where the mischief lies.
It worries me to know…' and then
'It worries me…' she said again.

'Perhaps if you could amplify
Your statement, child, I could
Draw from my wealth of wisdom I
Have never understood,
And juggling to and fro with it
Could give some angle that would fit.'

'O you are Old and full of years!
But haven't got a clue.
What use is solace to the fears
My soul is stumbling through.
Even that ornament of gold
Is quite enough to turn me cold.'

'Your thwarted and convulsive thought
Is mere child's-play to me
These mental wanderings are nought
But biblic fantasy.
You are a whimsy thing and do
Not understand what's good for you.'

'It's you who'll never understand.
You're ancient, cold and blind!'
He heard her turn, then felt a hand
Pluck at his socks behind.
Apparently she's on the floor,
He thought – What next? I'll speak to her.

From *Figures of Speech*. The Key to the drawing is on p. 234.

'Child, child, child, child, child, child,' he said,
'You must not be so prone
To scoff at someone else's head
Because it's not your own.
Your wishful dreams are gaunt and blue –
Your hand has blood upon it too.'

'My hand has blood upon it! O
What grizzly work is this!
What do you mean? It's white as snow –
The kind a prince might kiss.'
'A Figure, dear – of Speech,' he said.
It doesn't mean your hands are red.'

'I've always hated them, and now
You've brought them up again!'
'Brought what, my dear, I'll take a vow
I don't know what you mean.'
'Those Figures, sir, of Speech,' she cried,
Her eyes as wild as they were wide.

'I've known them all, and exorcized
As many as I could.
I've had the priest and he advised
I chopped down half the wood –
A lovely wood of oak it was
Whose branches creaked against my house.

'But it has gone and for a time
The Figures let me be.
Their Speech was all about a crime
I did when I was three.
And now you've let them loose once more.'
She rose and wandered to the door.

'O I must leave you now, and leave
You now for all my days.
Adieu. Adieu. My heart shall grieve
In multitudinous ways.
Though you may have your theories, I
Shall nurse a child named poetry.

'And those dynamic things that lie
Within a carrot's brain –
The passion of the wormwood fly
That grows against the grain –
If you were such as I you'd sing
The praises of a buzzard's wing.

'I will away! You are not of
My calibre or clay.
You grope down the provincial groove
And theorize all day.
You're old and clinical and can't
Accept me as a Simple Plant.'

There was no answer, for alas
The wise and cloudy man
Had, like a story come to pass
Directly it began,
And faded gently through the door
And she was left to hold the floor.

She held it bravely, till the pain
Of blisters at her palm
Forced her to leave its oaken grain
And wander to the farm.
The cattle moo'd, the byres were clean
But O, what did their psyche mean?

All flowers that die: all hopes that fade:
All birds that cease to cry:
All beds that vanish once they're made
To leave us high and dry –
All these and many more float past
Across the roofs of Gormenghast.

(c. 1949)

A-Lolling on the Shores of Old Hawaii

A-lolling on the shores of old Hawaii,
Never tryee
To understand.
The moon is up above us in the sky-ee –
As planned.

(1953)

O'er Seas that Have No Beaches

O'er seas that have no beaches
To end their waves upon,
I floated with twelve peaches,
A sofa, and a swan.

With flying-fish above me
And with cat-fish all around,
There was no one to love me
Nor hope of being found –

When, on the blurred horizon,
(So endlessly a-drip),
I saw – all of a sudden!
No sign… of any… ship.

(1953)

From *Figures of Speech*. The Key to the drawing is on p. 234.

The Bullfrog and the Flies

Once upon the Banks of a Green Stream
That was full of water… (*wet* water…)
There sat a Bullfrog;
And he was Vain as Vanity itself
And he had no rival.
And as for his eyes – they *rolled*;
And as for his ears – he hadn't any;
And as for his Voice – it was ripe as thunder!
And he loved Flies.
But his love was not the right kind of love
For he loved them only to eat them up!
But there was one Fly –
One especial Fly –
Who was the King of all the Flies,
(That lived on the banks of the Green Stream
That was full of water… (*wet* water)).
O yes… he was King of them all,
Because of his brains;
And his speech
And his brains
And his beauty
And his brains
And he called for a Meeting.
'Ladies and Gentlemen,' he began
(And his voice was sharper than needles)
'Stop buzzing and listen to me.'
And all the flies clapped their hands.
'No! no! not yet!' said the King Fly,
'Stand still and be quiet and Listen!'
And they became quiet, and they listened,
And all that they could hear
Was the Bullfrog in the next field
Who was hungry for more Flies.
'I have had an idea,' said the King Fly at last.
'Yes! yes!' cried the Flies.
'We shall whizz to the thornbush *now*!
Where the bright thorns grow.'
'Yes… yes…'
'Break off the thorns and stick them on our noses.'

'What for?' (said the Flies).
'For to puncture him with,' said the King Fly.
'After all… he has eaten up nearly all our friends.'
'Just Listen to him.'
'We look like unicorns!' said a Fly-Voice.
And they did: with thorns on their noses and their brows.
'Are we all ready?' said the King of the Flies.
'Then charge!'
And all at once they whizzed through the air
And pierced the Bullfrog in a hundred places
So that he exploded!
And there was no more Bullfrog to be seen.
Only his favourite patch of wet grass
Where he used to sit
On the banks of the Green Stream
And eat flies.

(1955)

The Rhino and the Lark

Once upon a time there was a Rhino –
Which is short for Rhinoserous –
And he had a Voice –
And what a Voice!!

It seemed to be made out of Rust
And grit and black sand,

And he was un-loved. (No wonder.)
Except for one little creature who had faith in him
And this little creature was a Skylark

Who wanted to save him from himself.

'Look here, my old wrinkled friend,'
Said the Skylark –
'We must defeat your horrid temper, mustn't we?'

'I don't know,' said the Rhino.

From *Figures of Speech*. The Key to the drawing is on p. 234.

'Come, come, we can talk more sweetly than *that*, can't we?'
Said the Skylark.

'I don't feel sweet,' said the Rhino.

'You certainly don't look sweet,' said the Skylark.
'But you must try.'

'I *have* been trying. And it's not fair,' said the Rhino.
'Why have you stuck that apple on the horn that's on my nose,
Eh! Just to tease me? Eh?'

'Because you love the taste of apples, don't you?'

'Supposing I do?'

'And it's made you very savage and horrid, hasn't it?'

'Supposing it has?'

'Well you know the way you try to bite it
With your savage mouth? And how you can't quite reach it?'

'Well?'

'Well I have a plan. A plan to make you patient.
Are you listening?'

'Supposing I am?'

'Then pay attention,' said the Skylark,
'Or you'll never have the beautiful red apple.
This is my plan.'

'Go on then,' said the Rhino.

'Well it's this.
Every morning when you wake up you will find a fresh green
apple
Stuck on the horn of your nose.'

'What for?'

'To make you control yourself
And to make you have loving thoughts.'

'Urgh,' said the Rhino.

'Then at luncheon time,' continued the Skylark,
'I will pluck the apple off your nose
(If you've been calm and quiet)
And you can eat it.'

'Oh.'

'But if you've been beastly and rude
I will leave the apple on your nose
Where you can't reach it.
Do you understand?'

'And how long will this go on for?' said the Rhino.
'It'll make me look so beastly foolish.'

'As soon as you've been gentle,' said the Skylark.
'After all *I'm* gentle, aren't I?
And I'm not nearly as big as you.'

'I don't think your *plan* is very gentle,' said the Rhino.
'And what has my size got to do with it?
But – I like apples.'

173

And do you know that Rhino did his best!
And his temper got sweeter and sweeter
Until he no longer had to have an apple on his nose at all.

How nice if all the other Rhinos in the world got gentler and
                                                                                             gentler
But I'm afraid they don't.
In fact most of them get worse and worse.

(c. 1955)

Richly in the Unctuous Dell

    Richly in the Unctuous Dell
    Where the dryads wallow,
    Not so dry as here-to-fore
    Half inclined to go before
    Half inclined to follow

    There the Patagonian queen,
    Glimmering like batter,
    Twice as rank as yesterday
    Half inclined to melt away
    Says it doesn't matter.

(early to mid 1950s)

Manifold Basket's Song

    Tiddle-ti-pompa,
    Tiddle-ti-pompa,
    Tiddle-ti-which-way,
    Tiddle-ti-pom –
    Dottle your eye-tles
    Crossle your tee-tles
    Bottle your beetles
    Tiddle-ti-pom…

(early to mid 1950s)

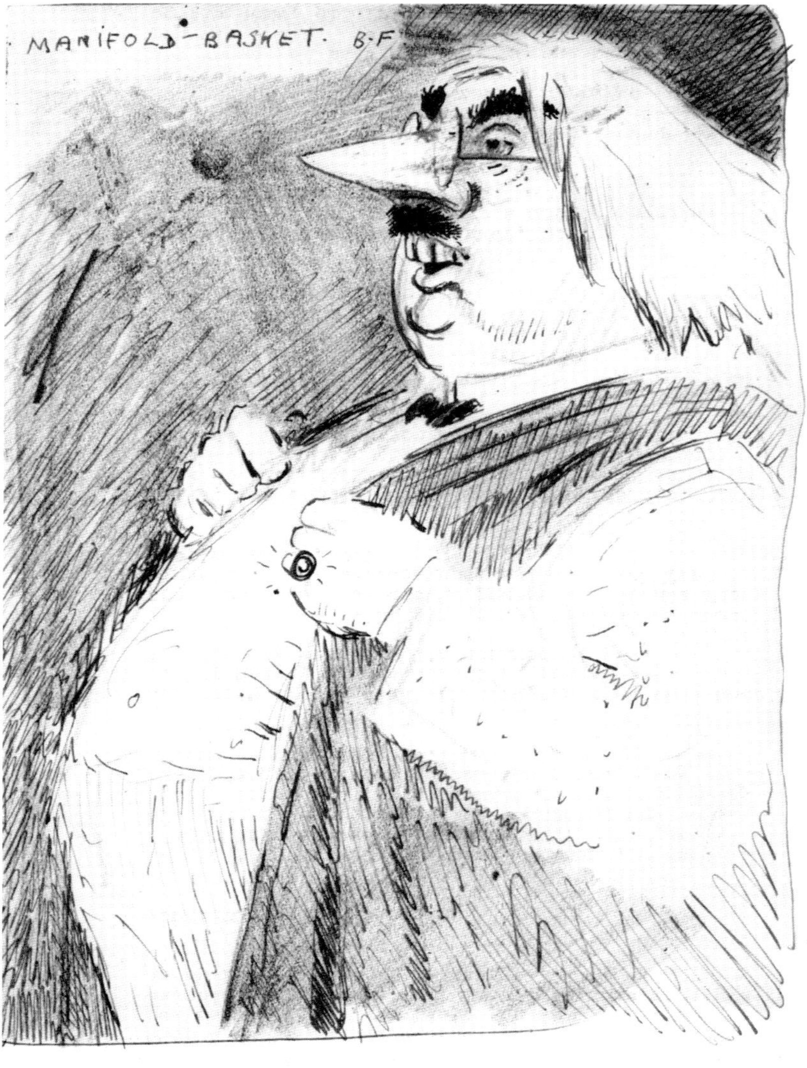
MANIFOLD-BASKET B.F

With a One, Two, Up!

With a one, two, up!
And a three, four, up!
Happy in the hayloft!
Happy as a pup!

With a four, five, down!
And a six, seven, down!
Plaster'd in the country,
Bottled in the town.

(c. 1953–7)

In Ancient Days

In ancient days, oh in ancient days,
In the land of Clink-a-doodle-ding,
I was warned by the Bishop for to mind my ways,
But I was a younker and the time was the spring,
So what could a younker-doodle do?
With his cod on fire and the sky so blue –
So what could a younker-doodle do?

(c. 1953–7)

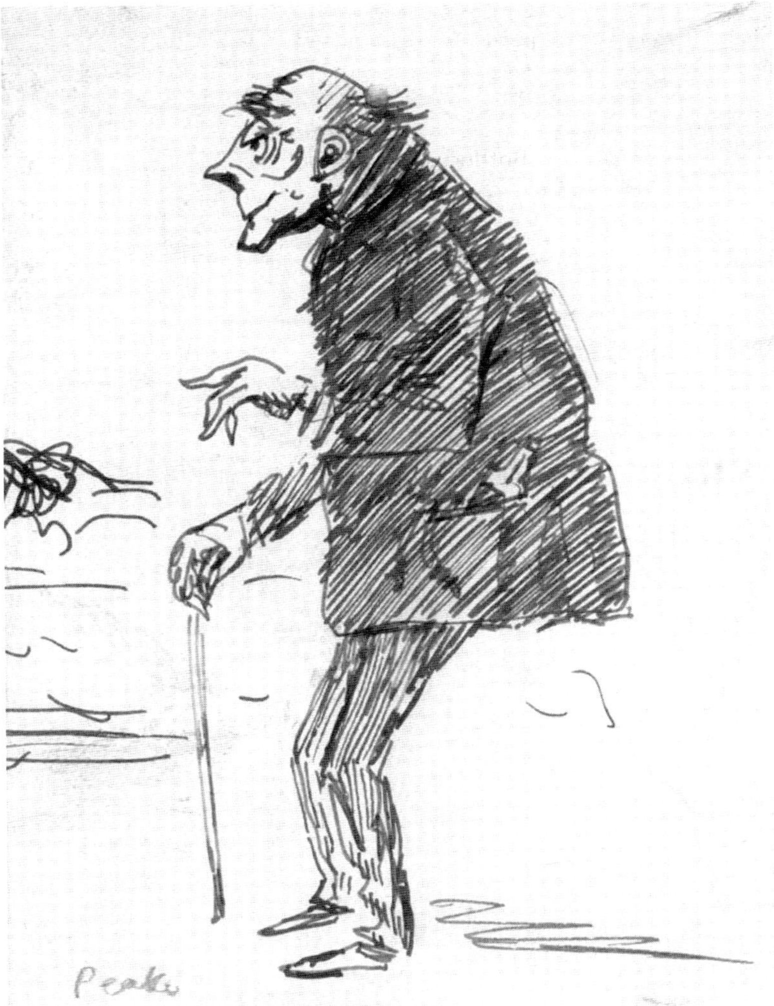
Peake

O Keep Away

O keep away
However much
The crops may need
Your lachrymose
And gentle touch
O you sweet rain
You irritating, melancholy rain

O keep away
However grey
The forecast is
This golden day
O you sweet rain,
You irritating, melancholy rain

(c. 1953–7)

O Darling When a Story's Done

Sally: O darling when a story's done,
Can we return to Chapter One
And find it green as grass?

Undertakers: And find it green as grass

Sally: Or can the clock unwind and tell
An earlier time, before we fell
Into this mood of strange 'alas',
This mood of pure 'alas'?

Undertakers: We do not know
We cannot tell

        (*A bell rings*)

We think that was
The dinner bell.

Away, away
Where sunbeams fail to play,
Away

And pass, and pass
Like spiders through the grass,
Alas.

We mourn. We mourn.
Our trouser-legs forlorn
Are torn –
        (*Exeunt Undertakers*)

(c. 1953–7)

Undertaker's Song (1)

(*The four undertakers move down to the floats where they go into a slow, shuffling dance to the accompaniment of strange music. Then, after humming the first note, one after the other, they join hands and sing –*)

>To our primordial calling
>We bring both guile and grace;
>(We know our place!)
>For what is more appalling
>Than fumbling in the face
>Of Daddy Death, our treasure-trove,
>Who loves to keep us on the move,
>(And in the groove)
>Heigh-ho! Heigh ho!
>The needle's in the groove.
>
>More, more, let us have more
>And more of these morbid mornings –
>More… more… than ever before
>Of these morticadaverous Warnings…
>Ever so care-ful, ever so slow –
>Down where the roots of the buttercups go…
>More… more… let us have more
>Of this lucrative Work of Woe.
>
>Woe… Woe…
>More of this Work of Woe.

(c. 1953–7)

Undertaker's Song (2)

1

Never look eager, friends
Never look spry
It isn't nice at all to show
The way one's feelings come and go
Never look eager
Never look spry.

Chorus: Alas poor Percy

2

Never look eager friends
Never look spry
It's Mr Percy's death, it is
And suicide's a dreadful biz
Never look eager
Never look spry

Chorus: Alas poor Percy

(c. 1953–7)

Nannie Slagg's Song

Never mind
Never mind
Let us see what we can find
One, two, and far away.

You look here
And I'll look there
Till we find the twisting stair
Three, four, and far away.

Mind the tread that isn't true
It will surely 'do' for you
Five, six and far-away.

(c. 1955)

Fuchsia's Song

All alone
All alone
Listening to the golden drone,
Golden drone,
Golden drone,
I am living all alone…

(c. 1955)

Nannie Slagg's Lullaby

Pretty heart be quiet, then
All the tigers have gone home,
Every beast is in his den,
Not a fly can do you harm,
Float away,
Float away,
Pretty one to dreamland.

(c. 1955)

Where the Little Dunderhead

Where the little dunderhead
Gobbled daisies with his bread
There is now a little grave
Teaching children to behave.

(c. 1955)

From *Figures of Speech*. The Key to the drawing is on p. 234.

Lean Sideways on the Wind

Lean sideways on the wind, and if it bears
Your weight you are a Daughter of the Dawn:
If not – pick up your carcass, dry your tears,
Brush down your dress – for that sweet elfin horn

You thought you heard was from no fairyland –
Rather it flooded through the kitchen floor,
From where your Uncle Eustace and his band
Of flautists turn my cellar, more and more

Into a place of hollow and decay:
That is my theory, darling, anyway.

(after 1957)

Of Pygmies, Palms and Pirates

Of pygmies, palms and pirates,
Of islands and lagoons,
Of blood-bespattered frigates,
Of crags and Octoroons,
Of whales and broken bottles,
Of quicksands cold and grey,
Of ullages and dottles,
I have no more to say.

Of barley, corn and furrows,
Of farms and turf that heaves
Above such ghostly burrows
As twitch on summer eves
Of fallow-land and pasture,
Of skies both pink and grey,
I made a statement last year
And have no more to say.

(after 1957)

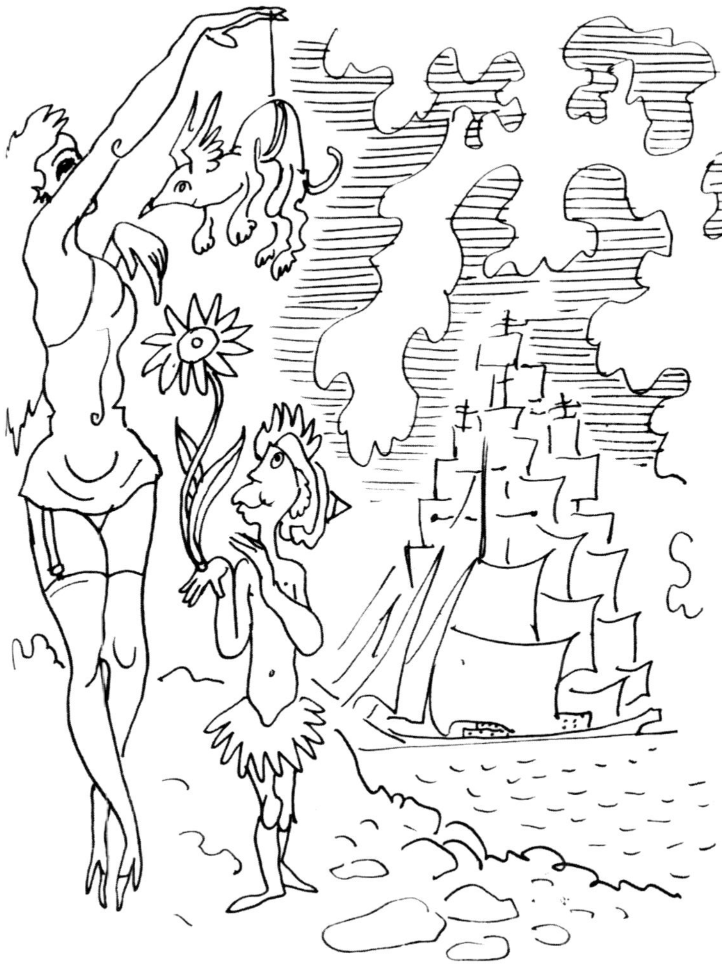

An Angry Cactus Does No Good

An angry cactus does no good
To flowers in a pensive mood
It riles them something horrible –
O wellaway – keep well away
The whole affair's deplorable
As one might say.

But take the humble spinach flower,
That lifts its whiskers to the shower
As 'twere a kind of benison
O welladay; keep well away –
It quotes the work of Tennyson,
The livelong day.

(after 1957)

I Cannot Give the Reasons

I cannot give the Reasons,
I only sing the Tunes:
The sadness of the Seasons,
The madness of the Moons.

I cannot be didactic
Or lucid, but I can
Be quite obscure and practic-
Ally marzipan

In gorgery and gushness
And all that's squishified
My voice has all the lushness
Of what I can't abide

And yet it has a beauty
Most proud and terrible
Denied to those whose duty
Is to be cerebral!

Among the antlered mountains
I make my viscous way
And watch the sepia fountains
Throw up their lime-green spray.

(after 1957)

From *Figures of Speech*. The Key to the drawing is on p. 234.

O Little Fly

O little fly! delightful fly!
Perch on my wrist again:
Then rub your legs and dry your eye,
And climb my fist again:

For surely, here, the atmosphere
Is somehow right and good for you.
I love you most, when as your host
I'm in the mood for you.

(after 1957)

How Fly the Birds of Heaven

How fly the birds of heaven save by their wings?
How tread the stags, those huge and hairy kings
Save by their feet? How do the fishes turn
In their wet purlieus where the mermaids yearn
Save by their tails? How does the plantain sprout
Save by that root it cannot do without?
I hope that I have made my meaning clear…

(after 1957)

From *Figures of Speech*. The Key to the drawing is on p. 234.

Leave the Stronger

Leave the stronger
And the lesser
Things to me!
Lest that Conger
Named Vanessa
Who is longer
Than a dresser
Visits thee

He is slippery,
He is hardy,
He is hardly ever
Tardy,
He can count
From one to three

Leave the stronger
And the lesser
Things to me!

(after 1957)

Fish or Fowl

Fish or fowl, it's all the same
To me, all's one – and two
And three
For I am now
Proclaimed and sworn
The sorriest cow
Of Capricorn

My scales are pink
My eyes are black
My feathers flutter
Down my back –
The firelight fails
To comfort me
All's one – all's two
And sometimes
Three.

(after 1957)

'Shrink! Shrink!'

'Shrink! Shrink!' said I
'But why?' she cried
'Do as I bid you,'
I replied

And as she once
Had promised she
Would both obey
And honour me

Just me! most just
And holy me
She shrank a bit
For me to see

'More! More!' I said
'That's not enough
I want you wrinkled up
Like duff

'For I am tired
Of your smooth skin
I want you wrinkled up
Like sin'

She then complied,
And when I saw
Her chin was tapping
On the floor

I said 'Enough!
Now you can go
To your Mamma
And tell her so.'

(after 1957)

An Old and Crumbling Parapet

An old and crumbling parapet
Arose out of the dancing sea –
And on its top there sat a flea
For reasons which I quite forget.

But as the sun descended, and
The moon uprose across the sky
We were alone, the flea and I,
And so I took it by the hand

And whispered, 'On your parapet
D'you think that there'd be room for me?'
'I cannot say,' replied the flea.
'I'm studying the Alphabet –'

But that was long ago, and Saints
Have died since then – and Ogres bled.
And purple tigers flopped down dead
Among the pictures and the paints.

(after 1957)

From *Figures of Speech*. The Key to the drawing is on p. 234.

It Is Most Best

It is most best,
Most *very* best,
To frown upon a welcome guest –
To frown and weep –
O lackaday!
Then to tie him to a hornet's nest
And steal away.

It may be he is nice
And mild
And welcome to a little child:
It well may be – O lackaday!
So leave him where
The wasps are wild,
And steal away.

(after 1957)

The Hours of Night Are Drawing On

The hours of night are drawing on
Their drawers of dark grey wool…
The hours of day are dead and gone
According to the rule

(after 1957)

From *Figures of Speech*. The Key to the drawing is on p. 234.

Over the Pig-Shaped Clouds They Flew

Over the pig-shaped clouds they flew
Eagles with eyes as dry as dew
And talons sharp as batter –
O very peculiar birds! they blew
From where? It doesn't matter.

(after 1957)

Come, Break the News to Me, Sweet Horse!

1

'Come, break the news to me, Sweet Horse
Do you not think it best?
Or if you'd rather not – of course
We'll let the matter rest.'

2

The biggest Horse that ever wore
His waistcoat inside out,
Replied: 'As I have sneezed before,
There's not a shade of doubt.'

3

'I find your answer rare, Sweet Horse,
Though hardly crystal clear,
But tell me true, what kind of course
Do you propose to steer?'

4

The biggest horse that ever wore
His waistcoat outside in –
Rolled over on the parquet floor,
And kissed me on the chin.

5

'O this is loveable,' I cried,
'And rather touching too,
Although I generally prefer
A lick of fish-bone glue.'

6

The only Horse who ever Kissed
Me smack athwart the chin
Curled up and died. He will be missed
By all who cherished Him.

(after 1957)

What Though My Jaw

What though my jaw be long and blue –
Were not the strong Toledo blades
Famous for this?
What though my nose be set askew
So are the Knives of Sheffield too
And proud of it

(after 1957)

The Trouble with Geraniums

The trouble with geraniums
Is that they're much too red!
The trouble with my toast is that
It's far too full of bread.

The trouble with a diamond
Is that it's much too bright:
The same applies to fish and stars,
And the electric light

The trouble with the crows I see
Lies in the way they fly;
The trouble with myself is all
Self-centred in the eye.

The trouble with my looking-glass
Is that it shows me, me:
There's trouble in all sorts of things
Where it should never be.

(after 1957)

Crocodiles

She stared at him as hard as she
Could stare, but not a single blush
Suffused his face like dawn at sea
Or roses in a bush –

For Crocodiles are very slow
At taking hints because their hide's
So thick it never feels *de trop*,
And tender like a bride's.

(after 1957)

Along the Cold, Regurgitating Shore

Along the cold, regurgitating
Shore we paced,
My arm around her irritating
Wasp-like waist…
She liked it so…

(after 1957)

I Have My Price

I have my price: it's rather high –
(About the level of your eye),
But if you're nice to me, I'll try
To lower it for you –
To lower it; to lower it;
Upon the kind of rope they knit
From yellow grass and purple hay
When knitting is taboo –

Some knit them pearl, some knit them plain –
Some knit their brows of pearl in vain
Some are so plain they try again
To tease the wool of love!
But ah! the palms of yesterday –
There's not a soul from yesterday
Who's worth the dreaming of – they say –
Who's worth the dreaming of…

(after 1957)

204

Jehovah, Jehovah

Jehovah, Jehovah,
Who landed at Dover
With a twelve foot beard
And a dog named Rover.

(late 1950s)

From *Figures of Speech*. The Key to the drawing is on p. 234.

From *Figures of Speech*. The Key to the drawing is on p. 234.

Synopsis
Over the Border
or
The Adventures of Footfruit

Footfruit, a healthy, happy man, crosses the border from the wilderness.

He is approached by an official, who seems to have risen out of the dust at his feet.

Far from interrogating Footfruit, the official becomes more and more fascinated by this happy creature and his answers. But he determines all the same to get him into the same mould as everyone else. Because they don't like people being different.

News spreads about him and more officials arrive. They are all agreed that they must do something about him; i.e. he has the wrong things on, and his nose is wrong, yet he was whistling and humming to himself. Only Footfruit's dog is passable. They cannot understand how he can be so ignorant, and yet so happy.

Why did he leave his home, they ask. He had after all enough food, drink and laughter.

'Adventure can be a voice.'
'A Voice?'
'Yes, in the night, my dear friends. I have been advised to leave the border, and stand upon the margin of civilization.'

Not only this, he wishes to prove himself to his tribe when he returns to the wasteland.

Footfruit can see in the darkness what looks like the outpost of a city. He leaps in the air with excitement. Is it not true that he is near to goodness, beauty and love? From now on he must believe all that he reads, sees or hears. He feels that his conversion is at hand. There is no time to waste.

Out strides Footfruit towards the distant city, leaving the officials far behind (including the dog).

Advertisements are from now on his Bible, and he will believe without question.

His religion is materialism. The hoardings dominate everything. An avenue of hoardings.

Taste.   Food he has been eating is natural, therefore must be bad. Taste-buds are sold in shops so that otherwise tasteless food can take on any flavour required.

Smell.   Natural smells are bad. Everything must be disguised. His nose grows big. Everyone stares at it on arrival. Also he has a natural odour which has to be got rid of.

Hearing.   Has been brought up to the sound of silence, or the natural ebullience of singing. Finds that music is potted and permanent, and if anyone is tasteless enough to sing on their own out of sheer *joie-de-vivre* they are sent to a reformatory where they are taught not to be anti-social. *As for my hearing… it is marvellously good. No one can spoil my privacy. Not now!*

Touch.   Civilized people don't *feel*.

Sight.   At first he couldn't see a thing, but later on he felt the Truth arriving, and he forced himself to benefit from all you stand for. It was a beautiful conception, and the dog loved it. As for the hoardings, they convinced me. There have been black moments of course, but what are they compared with this glory? O Science, what a lad you are.

Priests are the salesmen to whom one confesses not owning such and such an article. Absolution is given on the understanding that the penitent will purchase whatever he has confessed to not owning, etc.

Footfruit has a very long confession to make. His jaws begin to ache, and his legs grow shorter and shorter with pressure from above. But he knows that there is Truth to be apprehended.

By the time 'civilization' has done its worst with Footfruit he wants to go back to the wilderness. He is to be met by a delegation, and given a hero's welcome.

When they see him, they are shocked at his terrible appearance, but they are told by ambassadors of civilization that he has had a magnificent schooling and they are delighted with all he has done since he left the wilderness. It takes some time to convince them that what has happened to him is 'good', but high pressure talk wears them down, and they come to realize that perhaps after all Footfruit is lucky. And they decide that they would like to follow in his footsteps.

The Adventures of Footfruit
or
The Enthusiast

Look!
Look!
Here cometh Footfruit, out of the wilderness: a fire in his belly, a purpose in his head; and a nose for the truth.
Exactly.
See how he covers the ground! Hey Footfruit! Footfruit!
Where are you off to now? Whizz! Bang! What a lad he is.
Can it be that he is making tracks for the border?

Yes, yes, and more than yes. He is heading for the City itself.
Ha! ha! ha! Ho! ho! ho! If only he knew.
What?
Oh never mind.
But tell me, why the agitation, my friend?
That is quite a question.
Let us watch him. All will unfold… we hope.
Thank heaven we're in hiding.
Thank heaven indeed.
Where is he now?
Yes, yes, yes. Where is he now.
I've spotted him. Aha! He moves like a God.

Step out Foot-Print, the world's
spread out before you: your failures
trail behind you + in the middle, why
there you are, my dear, with ears like
worm-casts.

Lo! here he comes at last:
along with that vile hound that dogs him.
Jackpot by name. He irks me.

Secretly — but secretly, let
me tell you something. I would rather be
training Jackpot than acting as a
kind of off-stage voice. In other words
I'm jealous. For he is a great man
with a great heart is Foot-Print.
(and he has big feet too.) What
more I would be near him, wouldn't I?
if I were Jackpot + perhaps, who knows,
one day... (the stomach turns, picturing
it) — I might touch him.
Water! water! with a touch

Which God?
O any good God… hallo there, he's disappeared again. Who would have thought it.
He's half way to the Border. Was ever man more ardent.
Or with better reason.
Aha…
For he is of the missionary breed.
As for the Border, each footfall brings him closer.
Heigh ho, heigh ho, and the high hills hoary.

Are you listening?
Why of course.
Very well then.
Yes, yes.
What is it that he carries in his hand – that powerful hand, gnarled by long usage? Can it be a document?
It can.
It is.
Carry it high then, Footfruit, as you stride. It is your passport into paradise.
Are you there?
Yes, indeed.
Some say good old Footfruit, but there are others. For my part I see in him the world's last hope, but what was that?
Only that mangy hound of his. Oh I could whip him to within an inch of his tail.
And now the rain. Does Footfruit care?
Not a jot.

See how his boots spout water.
See how he laughs. Ha ha!
As though he had no care in all the world. Footfruit the great.
Footfruit the glorious.
No doubt of it.
For see, his future spread before him, his past spread out behind him; and in the middle, why there is our friend indeed, with his warrior's head, and his ears like worm-casts.
Sweet Footfruit! There is no question of it, for he's both sweet and great.

Why otherwise should he dream.
Dream?
Yes, dream. Dream of Doing Good. Wherefore his passion to leave the wilderness which was his home?
It is hard to fathom. He does not know himself. All he knows is that shortly after dawn this splendid morning, he heard the call, and he upped and he went.
Confound that dog of his.
He laughs like a drain.

Forget him.
I will try to.
Aha Footfruit. He believes that everyone is there to do him good.
I know.
Just as he is ready to do good to everyone.
He knows very well that the Great City is far away, yet he strides out like a madman.
Or as though he had a tiger on his tail.
Time was when Footfruit spurned the twisting globe. All of it. No quarter asked; none given. As a spurner there were few to touch him. And those who did soon took their feet away.
Do you remember those days?
I do indeed. Why, civilization itself came within the range of his lash.
His gentle lash.
As you say, his gentle lash.
And the Cities were like gall-spots on his tongue. But now he knows better. Civilization was alright.
Quite alright.
And the cities were alright.
As you say.
Do you agree?
Yes, yes. But watch that filthy hound. I have him in the corner of my eye. Heigh ho, heigh ho. He had heard stories.
And he had had inklings.
Goat's milk and locusts.
He had put two and two together with outrageous results.
He had been seen, leaning across the dawn, dreaming of the Big City.
He was undoubtedly touched.
No, no.
No? He had an independence of spirit, that is all.
There he goes… there's no holding him.
Oh what a glorious, uproarious, bounding beast he is.
Oh what a pride he takes in every stride he makes.
What a splendid picture, Footfruit and his hound, I must admit it. They carve themselves in air.
Hang on Footfruit. This is the real thing. Strap on your breastplate!
Flair the proud nostril, blare out in your extreme abandon.
The truth, my friend, and nothing but the truth.

(c. 1957–60)

Another Draft of Footfruit

How otherwise can I unfold myself and the affairs of Footfruit. And his dog.

    Let me make a confession – I have never met him or been introduced. But I have followed his career, & once I smelt the tang of his cigar. So I was fairly near him when I have followed him to his next

Chapter 1

Here cometh Footfruit, head-foremost, bum backmost; Chapter 1, Verse 1 – heigh ho… heigh ho… and the high hills hoary:

Footfruit! Footfruit! Where are you? He has fire in his blood has Footfruit and a nose for the Truth. (This can be awkward.)

What, no reply? Is this a time to tease your Chronicler? Really, Footfruit: the whole thing's about as chronic as it could be! Ha ha ha… sh… sh…

Step out Footfruit, the world's spread before you; your failures trail behind you & in the *middle*, why there *you* are, my dear, with ears like worm-casts.

Lo! Here he comes at last: along with that vile hound that dogs him. Jackpot by name. He irks me.
Secretly – but *secretly*, let me tell you something. I would rather be trailing Jackpot than acting as a kind of off-stage Voice. In other words I'm jealous. For he is a great man with a great heart is Footfruit. (And he has big feet too). What's more I would be *near* him, wouldn't I? if I were Jackpot & perhaps, who knows, one day … (the stomach turns, picturing it) — I might *touch* him.
Water! Water!

(c. 1957–60)

From *Figures of Speech*. The Key to the drawing is on p. 234.

Crown Me with Hairpins

Crown me with hairpins intertwined
Into a wreath each hairpin lined
With plush that only spinsters find
At night beneath huge sofas where
The feathers, wool, and straw and hair
Bulge through a lining old as time
And secret as a beldam's lair
Of ghostly grime.

Tired aunts who live on sphagnum moss
Are quite the best to ask, because
They are less likely to get cross
Than those less ancient ones who still
Peer coyly from the window-sill,
Until their seventieth year.
Go find an old and *tired* one,
Secure the hairpin; then have done
With your relations, dear.

Notes

Abbreviations

For full publication details see 'References and Further Reading', p. 16.

Batchelor	Batchelor, *Mervyn Peake: A Biographical and Critical Exploration*
BN	Peake, *A Book of Nonsense*
Bod. Dep. Peake 16	Undated exercise book entitled 'Nonsence Poems'; see Introduction, p. 2. Now in the Peake archive at the British Library, reference Add. MS 88931.
f.p.	first published
G	Peake, *Gormenghast*
MB	Peake's unfinished play *Manifold Basket*, written early to mid-1950s.
MP	Peake, *Mr Pye*
MPR	*Mervyn Peake Review*
N1	1939 notebook (see Introduction, p. 1, and Peake, *Collected Poems*, pp. 1–2). Now in the Peake archive at the British Library, reference Add. MS 88931.
N2	1946 notebook (see Introduction, p. 1, and Peake, *Collected Poems*, pp. 1–2). Now in the Peake archive at the British Library, reference Add. MS 88931.
Nonsence 1	1947 Nonsence notebook (see Introduction, p. 1). Now in the Peake archive at the British Library, reference Add. MS 88931.
Nonsence 2	Post-1957 Nonsence notebook (see Introduction, pp. 1–2). Now in the Peake archive at the British Library, reference Add. MS 88931.
Peake Archive	Reference Add. MS 88931 in the British Library
PP	Peake, *Peake's Progress*, 1981 edition
PS	*Peake Studies*
RWR	Peake, *Rhymes without Reason*
Smith	Smith, *Mervyn Peake: A Personal Memoir*
TA	Peake, *Titus Alone* (TA 1 refers to the first edition, TA 2 the second – see 'Further Reading', p. 16)
TG	Peake, *Titus Groan*
VH	Winnington, *The Voice of the Heart*
W&D	Peake, *Writings and Drawings*
WW	Peake's play *The Wit to Woo*, first performed in 1957
Yorke	Malcolm Yorke, *Mervyn Peake: My Eyes Mint Gold*

Notes

p. 21   'I Saw a Puffin': f.p. Batchelor, p. 79, where the conjectural date is given. Written with Peake's brother Leslie. Source unknown.

p. 22   'The Song of Lien Tsung': f.p. *PS*, vol. 2, no. 4 (Summer 1992), pp. 25–6, along with its source, a letter to Gordon Smith dated 25 January 1930. In that year Peake began writing a light opera which he summarized to Smith as follows: 'an Emperor, his beautiful daughter (*à la carte*) the Captain of the Guard (in love with The Emp's daughter) soldiers etc, & the Chinese pirate bandits, who live in a cave up in the hills. All in China of course.

'The Captain of the Guard is found wooing the Emp's daughter and chucked out. He then becomes a bandit & rises in the ranks. The Emp's daughter is captured as a hostage, and cannot be ransomed, the price being too high. So she is to be beheaded next Thursday – oh weladay – etc. Lien Tsung the hero bandit, (incidently the name of our last Coolie in Tientsin) he saves of course, & then I presume the conventional ending. But the plot doesn't matter in Light Opera – mine is so light that it probably won't exist.

'This is the Song of Lien Tsung, the first verse of it, that is, that he sings when cast from the Emperor's court.'

p. 23   'Waddon': unpublished. Source: MS on the front endpaper of a copy of *TG*, now owned by Jim Boyd, scanned for us by his daughter Madeleine. Date given by Pete Bellotte in his article 'Did You Know…?', *PS*, vol. 2, no. 4 (Summer 1992), pp. 18–28. According to Lady Patricia Masefield (speaking to Pete Bellotte in 1989), while a student at the Royal Academy Schools Peake would 'travel up to town by train and make rhymes about the stations'. This is the first of five surviving 'Railway Ditties'.

p. 23   'Thornton Heath': f.p. *PS*, vol. 2, no. 4 (Summer 1992), p. 20. Source: MS on the front endpaper of a copy of *TG*, now owned by Jim Boyd, scanned for us by his daughter Madeleine. This is one of the 'Railway Ditties'; for date and other details, see note to 'Waddon', above.

p. 23   'Norbury': f.p. *PS*, vol. 2, no. 4 (Summer 1992), p. 20. Source: MS on the front endpaper of a copy of *TG*, now owned by Jim Boyd, scanned for us by his daughter Madeleine. This is one of the 'Railway Ditties'; for date and other details, see note to 'Waddon', above.

p. 23   'Streatham and Balham': f.p. Yorke, p. 212. Source: MS on the front endpaper of a copy of *TG*, now owned by Jim Boyd, scanned for us by his daughter Madeleine. This is one of the 'Railway Ditties'; for date and other details, see note to 'Waddon', above.

p. 24   'Green Park': unpublished. Source: supplied by Pete Bellotte from a letter to Gordon Smith in his possession, dated 14 August 1930. This confirms the date we have assigned to the other four 'Railway Ditties', for which see note to 'Waddon', above.

p. 24   'You Can Never Be Sure of Your Birron': unpublished. Source: supplied by Pete Bellotte from an undated letter to Gordon Smith in his possession. Date conjectural, based on period when Peake worked with Gordon Smith on a book called *The Dusky Birron*.

p. 26   'Beard of My Chin': unpublished. Source: Peake archive MS, on the same leaf that contains 'You Before Me' (below). Date conjectural, based on period when Peake worked with Gordon Smith on *The Moccus Book*, which features the plains of Phiz. Some punctuation has been added.

p. 26 'You Before Me': unpublished. Source: Peake archive MS. Date conjectural, based on the dating of 'Beard of My Chin' (above), which occurs in the same MS. There is a longer version of this poem in Bod. Dep. Peake 16, pp. 13^r–14^r.

p. 26 'Although I Love Him': unpublished. Source: Peake archive MS, on the same leaf that contains 'You Before Me' and 'Beard of My Chin'. Date conjectural, based on the dating of 'Beard of My Chin (see note, above).

p. 29 'Practically Poetry': f.p. *Satire*, December 1934, p. 17, which is our source and supplies the date.

p. 30 'Ode to a Bowler': f.p. *Satire*, December 1934, p. 17, which is our source and supplies the date. This is the first of several poems featuring bowlers. See 'Tintinnabulum' and 'The Men in Bowler Hats Are Sweet' (pp. 128, 148).

p. 31 'Raft Song of the *Conger Eel*': f.p. *PP*, pp. 83–4, which is our source and supplies the date. The song is sung by the piratical crew of Mr Slaughterboard's ship as they paddle towards an island. The following commentary occurs between the stanzas: 'For all the unlovely content of the song, one might imagine judging from Mr Croozle Zenith's face that he were conducting some gentle lullaby. Never so happy in the world was Mr Zenith as when leading these creatures [i.e. the pirates] in song. The songs were varied. Their words were the outcome of age-old snatches bandied here and there in the dim piratical past, slowly evolved among the crews of buccaneer ships the seas over. Now their form was fixed as it were in a vice of all the hirsute throats that sang or rather roared this Raft Song of the *Conger Eel*; none more delicately expressed its sentiments and appreciated its nonsense than Slaughterboard. To most of the pirates it was as a germ in their blood, it was part of their life. To Mr Slaughterboard it was as the nursery rhyme is to the scholar. A thing to be wondered at, a thing that denied analysis by a sort of inevitability of wording and form.'

p. 35 'The Dwarf of Battersea': f.p. *BN*, pp. 13–21. Source: in the absence of the MS, apart from the first five stanzas reproduced in *BN*, p. 16, we have followed the text printed in *BN*, which gives the date. In the MS, the refrain 'Sing you-O, to me-O' is different in each stanza (with and without a comma, with and without dashes); we have normalized it throughout. The line 'But he has now passed over see' in the last stanza leaves us in a quandary: is 'see' a misreading of 'sea', or is it a pun for 'But he has now passed over [i.e., he is dead], [do you] see?' In doubt, we have left the line as it is. Date: in her introduction to *BN*, Maeve Gilmore describes the genesis of the poem as follows: 'In early 1937 [Peake] rented an ex-barber's shop in Battersea Church Road, which he used as a studio. The house, No. 163, now about to be demolished, is very close to a church which Blake, whom he so admired, frequented. It was at No. 163 Battersea Church Road that he gave me, before we were married, an envelope. Inside, in a beautiful longhand, was "The

223

Dwarf of Battersea", the first poem he ever wrote for me.'

p. 42 'Thank God for a Tadpole': unpublished. Source: N1, unpaginated section. Date given in MS. A full stop has been omitted at line 3.

p. 42 'About My Ebb and Flow-ziness': unpublished. Source: N1, unpaginated section; hence the conjectural date. This is the first of several instances of Peake playing with ebbing and flowing; see 'A Fair Amount of Doziness' (p. 43), 'My Uncle Paul of Pimlico' (p. 86), and 'I Waxes and I Wanes, Sir' (p. 100). Similarly, in *TG* Nannie Slagg complains to Dr Prunesquallor: 'I ebbs and I flows, sir […] and I falls away like' (p. 400).

p. 43 'A Fair Amount of Doziness': unpublished. Source: N1, unpaginated section; hence the conjectural date. See note to 'About My Ebb and Flow-ziness', above.

p. 44 'Ancient Root O Ancient Root': unpublished. Source: N1, unpaginated section; hence the conjectural date. These lines anticipate the longer poem about 'The Hideous Root' (p. 140). 'Root' has been a slang term for the penis since the sixteenth century.

p. 44 'The Frivolous Cake': f.p. *TG*, pp. 70–1, which is our source. An early draft is in N1 (where the cause of the flying crumbs is a wound made by the knife); hence the conjectural date. The first four lines of the third stanza form the first four lines of 'All Over The Lilac Brine!' (p. 78), with one small change. The poem recalls Charles E. Caryll's pirate song 'A Capital Ship' from *Davy and the Goblin* (1886); see G. Peter Winnington, 'Parodies and Poetical Allusions', *PS*, vol. 7, no. 4 (April 2002), pp. 25–9. In *TG*, p. 70, Fuchsia reads it in 'a big coloured book of verses and pictures', where it is 'a great favourite' of hers. For another poem from the book see 'Simple, Seldom and Sad' (p. 47).

p. 47 'Simple, Seldom and Sad': f.p. *TG*, p. 128, which is our source. There is a draft in N1 – hence our date – and another version in *RWR*; see 'Sensitive, Seldom and Sad' (p. 106), and note. In *TG*, Steerpike reads the poem in Fuchsia's 'large hand-painted book' of pictures and verses (see 'The Frivolous Cake' note, above).

p. 48 'Linger Now with Me, Thou Beauty': f.p. *TG*, pp. 119–20, which is our source. Date given in MS of *TG*. In *TG* the verses are recited by the Castle Poet; for another poem by him, see 'Song of the Castle Poet' (p. 156). In 1937 an obscure American poet, Mabel Ingalls Wescott, published some verses beginning 'Let me linger by the trellis' which borrow phrases, the trochaic rhythm, and the 'old fifteener' line from Tennyson's 'Locksley Hall'. In 'Linger Now with Me, Thou Beauty' Peake uses the same metre and repeats Wescott's key verb, 'to linger' (which is not prominent in Tennyson, nor is there any hint in Peake's poem that he was aware of 'Locksley Hall'). It seems improbable that Peake should be parodying Ms Wescott's lines, yet passages in his play *WW* also echo her poem. For more on this, see *VH*, pp. 270–1.

p. 50 'I Married Her in Green': unpublished. Source: MS of *TG*, where the date is given. It is not clear that the last two stanzas bear any relation to the first four, nor whether they were intended to be placed in any particular order.

p. 53 'Swelter's Song': f.p. *PS*, vol. 7, no. 2 (April 2001), pp. 5–8. Source: MS of *TG*, where the date is given. This is the song Swelter promises but never delivers in the published edition of *TG*, p. 30. He describes it as 'An old shong of great shadness' (p. 28), 'a shong to a hard-hearted monshter' and 'a dirgeous mashterpeesh' (p. 29).

p. 58 'I Cannot Simply Stand and Watch': unpublished. Source: MS of *TG*, where the date is given. Question mark and quotation marks added at line 8.

p. 59 'Upon the Summit of a Hill': unpublished. Source: MS of *TG*, where the date is given. Full stop added at line 4.

p. 60 'Come, Sit Beside Me Dear, He Said': unpublished. Source: Bod. Dep. Peake 16, pp. 9^v–12^r. On the other side of 12 is an early draft of 'Linger Now with Me, Thou Beauty', with no reference to Gormenghast. The date of 'Linger Now' supplies the conjectural date of this poem. Punctuation has been added as follows: a full stop at stanza 2, line 5, and a quotation mark at line 6; in stanza 3, a full stop at line 2, quotation marks and a comma at line 3, and a full stop at line 6; in stanza 4, commas at lines 2 and 4; in stanza 5, a dash at line 4; a full stop at the end of stanza 6; in stanza 7, a dash at line 3, a comma at line 4, a full stop at the end; in stanza 8, full stops at lines 2 and 6; in stanza 9, full stops at lines 2 and 6, a comma at line 3 and a colon at line 4.

p. 63 'Deliria': unpublished. Source: Bod. Dep. Peake 16, pp. 1^r–2^r. This is an early version of 'The Camel' (p. 96); hence the date. In addition, p. 1^r of the MS contains part of an early draft of 'All Over the Lilac Brine!', which reads as follows: 'Around the shores of the Arrogant Isles / Where the catfish bask and purr / I skim alone in a boat that I made'. An inverted comma has been added in stanza 11, line 2, and full stops at the end of stanzas 1, 2 and 6.

p. 64 'The Sunlight Lies Upon the Fields': unpublished. Source: Bod. Dep. Peake 16, p. 2^v. This is a draft of 'The Sunlight Falls Upon the Grass' (p. 80); hence the date.

p. 65 'Mine Was the One': unpublished. Source: Bod. Dep. Peake 16, p. 3^r. This contains elements of the poem 'What a Day It's Been!' (p. 90), and the paper on which it is written is clearly from the same source as 'Deliria' (p. 63); hence the date. An opening quotation mark has been added at the beginning of stanza 3, because Peake gives a closing quotation mark at stanza 3, line 4, thus implying that the whole stanza is direct speech. It's equally possible, of course, that *all* of the first three stanzas are direct speech; the reader may choose.

p. 68 'The Threads of Thought Are Not for Me': unpublished. Source: Bod. Dep. Peake 16, p. 3^v. The paper on which the MS is written is clearly from same source as 'Deliria' (p. 63); hence the conjectural date. For another thread poem, see 'The Threads Remain' (p. 123). The term 'whisky priest' in stanza 4 was first used by Peake's friend Graham Greene in *The Power and the Glory* (1940).

p. 69 'Come Husband! Come, and Ply the Trade': unpublished. Source: Bod. Dep. Peake 16, pp. 4^r–4^v. The paper on which the MS is written is clearly from same source as 'Deliria' (p. 63); hence the conjectural date.

p. 71 'How Good It Is to Be Alone (1)': unpublished. Source: Bod. Dep. Peake 16, pp. 2^r–2^v. The paper on which it is written is clearly from same source as 'Deliria' (p. 63), which gives the date. This is a version – probably an early draft – of 'How Good It Is to Be Alone (2)' (p. 73).

See the note to that poem (below); and also the note to 'My Uncle Paul of Pimlico' (below).

p. 73 'How Good It Is to Be Alone (2)': f.p. *PP*, p. 491. Source: Bod. Dep. Peake 16, p. 8ʳ. On the other side of the MS is an early draft of 'Sensitive, Seldom and Sad', which supports the date. This seems to be the more definitive version of the poem; drafts of it are scribbled round the edges of version 1. Full stops have been added at the end of stanzas 1 and 2. See note to 'My Uncle Paul of Pimlico' (below).

p. 76 'Upon My Golden Backbone': f.p. *RWR*, p. 8, which is our source and gives the date.

p. 78 'All Over the Lilac Brine!': f.p. *RWR*, p. 10, which is our source and gives the date. The first four lines of the poem repeat 'The Frivolous Cake', stanza 3 (p. 45), with one small change.

p. 80 'The Sunlight Falls upon the Grass': f.p. *RWR*, p. 12, which is our source and gives the date. A draft of the poem is given above as 'The Sunlight Lies Upon the Fields' (p. 64).

p. 82 'The Crocodile': f.p. *RWR*, p. 14, which is our source and gives the date.

p. 84 'The Giraffe': f.p. *RWR*, p. 16, which is our source and gives the date.

p. 86 'My Uncle Paul of Pimlico': f.p. *RWR*, p. 18, which is our source and gives the date. See note to 'About My Ebb and Flow-ziness' (p. 224). This is the first of a number of Uncle and Aunt poems Peake wrote throughout his career; see 'What a Day It's Been!' (p. 90), 'How Good It Is to Be Alone' (1) and (2) (pp. 71, 73), 'The Threads Remain' (p. 123), 'Aunts and Uncles' (p. 150), 'Lean Sideways On the Wind' (p. 186), and 'Crown Me With Hairpins' (p. 220).

p. 88 'It Makes a Change': f.p. *RWR*, p. 20, which is our source and gives the date.

p. 90 'What a Day It's Been!': f.p. *RWR*, p. 22, which is our source and gives the date. Part of stanza 3 is echoed in the poem 'Mine Was the One' (p. 65), and the last two lines are repeated in 'I Must Begin to Comprehend' and 'The Threads Remain' (pp. 122, 123). See also note to 'My Uncle Paul of Pimlico' (above).

p. 92 'How Mournful to Imagine': f.p. *RWR*, p. 24, which is our source and gives the date.

p. 94 'The Jailor and the Jaguar': f.p. *RWR*, p. 26, which is our source and gives the date.

p. 96 'The Camel': f.p. *RWR*, p. 28, which is our source and gives the date. A longer version of the poem is given above as 'Deliria' (p. 63). For the poem's debt to Wordsworth see G. Peter Winnington, 'Parodies and Poetical Allusions', *PS*, vol. 7, no. 4 (April 2002), pp. 25–9.

p. 98 'I Wish I Could Remember': f.p. *RWR*, p. 30, which is our source and gives the date.

p. 100 'I Waxes and I Wanes, Sir': f.p. *RWR*, p. 32, which is our source and gives the date. See note to 'About My Ebb and Flow-ziness' (p. 224).

p. 102 'The Hippopotamus': f.p. *RWR*, p. 34, which is our source and gives the date.

p. 104 'A Languorous Life': f.p. *RWR*, p. 36, which is our source and

gives the date.
- p. **106** 'Sensitive, Seldom and Sad': f.p. *RWR*, p. 38, which is our source and gives the date. For another version of the poem see 'Simple, Seldom and Sad' (p. 47). When Peake gave Gordon Smith a painting called 'The Sea-Weed Gatherers', depicting three men beside a yellowish sea, he explained that 'the fronds of coloured weed they hold and admire […] are poetry' (Smith p. 42). The symbolism may apply to this poem.
- p. **108** 'Roll Them Down': unpublished. Source: N2, p. 63; hence the conjectural date.
- p. **110** 'One Day When They Had Settled Down': f.p. *PS*, vol. 5 no. 4 (April 1998), p. 21. Source: Bonham's catalogue for the sale of this text, with its accompanying image, on 16 December 1997. Date given in catalogue. One of five poems commissioned by Henry Hobhouse for publication in a new monthly magazine called *Outlook*, which never materialized.
- p. **112** 'Again! Again! and Yet Again': f.p. *PS*, vol. 5, no. 4 (April 1998), p. 22. Source: Bonham's catalogue for the sale of this text, with its accompanying image, on 16 December 1997. Date given in catalogue. This is one of five poems commissioned by Henry Hobhouse for publication in a new monthly magazine called *Outlook*, which never materialized.
- p. **113** 'Uncle George': f.p. *PS*, vol. 5, no. 4 (April 1998), p. 23. Source: Bonham's catalogue for the sale of this text, with its accompanying image, on 16 December 1997. See note to 'My Uncle Paul of Pimlico' (p. 226). Date given in catalogue. Full stop added at end of poem. This is one of five poems commissioned by Henry Hobhouse for publication in a new monthly magazine called *Outlook*, which never materialized.
- p. **114** 'The King of Ranga-Tanga-Roon': f.p. *PS*, vol. 5, no. 4 (April 1998), p. 24. Source: Bonham's catalogue for the sale of this text, with its accompanying image, on 16 December 1997. Date given in catalogue. This is one of five poems commissioned by Henry Hobhouse for publication in a new monthly magazine called *Outlook*, which never materialized.
- p. **115** 'I Cannot Give You Reasons': f.p. *PS*, vol. 5, no. 4 (April 1998), p. 27. Source: Bonham's catalogue for the sale of this text, with its accompanying image, on 16 December 1997. Date given in catalogue. This is one of five poems commissioned by Henry Hobhouse for publication in a new monthly magazine called *Outlook*, which never materialized.
- p. **116** 'The Ballad of Sweet Pighead': unpublished. Source: Bod. Dep Peake 16, pp. 17^r–20^r. Date given in MS. Punctuation altered as follows: comma at end of stanzas 1 and 2, line 1. Stanza 2, line 2: full stop, and line 3: comma. Stanza 3: commas removed after 'human' and asylum'. Stanza 4: full stop added at line 2, commas at line 3 and end of line 4. Full stop added at end of stanza 5. Full stop added at stanza 6, line 2. Stanza 8: comma added at end of line 1. Stanza 9: comma added at end of line 1, full stop at end of stanza. Stanzas 12 and 13: full stop added at line 2. Full stop added at end of stanza 13. Stanza 14: comma added at line 2. Stanza 15: comma added at end of line 1. Stanza 16: two commas added at line 1, one at line 2. Stanza 17: full stop and inverted

comma added at end. Stanza 18: inverted commas added at line 3, comma after 'mother', full stop at end of stanza. Stanza 19: inverted comma and comma added at line 1; full stop (replacing semi-colon), inverted comma and capital at line 3; full stop at end of stanza. Stanza 20: inverted comma and two commas added at line 1; dash added (in place of comma) at line 3, comma at end of stanza. Stanza 21: inverted comma added at beginning; commas removed after 'answer' and added after 'found'; ellipsis and inverted comma added at end of poem.

p. 120 'Hold Fast': f.p. *G*, pp. 117–18, which is our source. An early version of this poem occurs in Nonsence 1, p. 8^v; hence the conjectural date. We have made one change on the strength of another MS in Peake's hand: in line 26 a full stop has been removed after 'thrush'.

p. 122 'I Must Begin to Comprehend': unpublished. Source: Peake Archive MS. The date is conjectural, based on the date of the version entitled 'The Threads Remain' (below). The last two lines repeat those of 'What a Day It's Been!' (p. 90). See also note to 'My Uncle Paul of Pimlico' (p. 226).

p. 123 'The Threads Remain': f.p. *BN*, p. 78. Source: Nonsence 1, p. 36^r; hence our conjectural date. We have deviated from the source at line 14: Nonsence 1 gives 'a man' in place of 'who's bred', but we have preferred the *BN* reading here. The poem is a version of 'I Must Begin to Comprehend' (p. 122). The last two lines repeat those of 'What a Day It's Been!' (p. 90).

p. 124 'White Mules at Prayer': this version f.p. *PS*, vol. 7, no. 1 (November 2000), pp. 20–1. Shorter versions were published in the first two editions of *TA*; see *TA 1* p. 38 (where we are told 'It was obvious that the poem was still in its early stages'), and *TA 2*, p. 42. (For the first edition Peake removed the first four stanzas of the poem at the suggestion of Maurice Temple Smith, his editor at Eyre & Spottiswoode, who felt it was too long.) Source: the MS of *G*, dated April–May 1949, where it is sung to Rottcodd, the keeper of the Hall of the Bright Carvings, by his mother. Date: another shorter draft occurs in Nonsence 1, pp. 35^r–35^v and p. 8^v; hence the conjectural date. In stanza 12 we have removed 'who' after 'spurs' to preserve the metre and added a comma at the end of the line; we have also added a comma after 'skull' in stanza 13. Both of these changes are based on the Nonsence 2 draft, which is in Peake's hand.

p. 127 'O Love, O Death, O Ecstasy': f.p. *BN*, p. 45, in a version based on Nonsence 2, p. 16^v, with another poem ('Along the Cold, Regurgitating Shore', p. 204) accidentally added to it. Source: Peake archive MS. Date: A draft of 'White Mules at Prayer' (p. 124) is on the reverse of the MS; hence the conjectural date. Note the occurrence of rhubarb by the sea in both poems. An exclamation mark has been added at stanza 2, line 2.

p. 128 'Tintinnabulum': f.p. *BN*, pp. 51–8. Source: Nonsence 1, pp. 1^r–3^v; hence the conjectural date. Punctuation has been added as follows: stanza 1, comma added at line 1; stanza 3, comma added at line 2; stanza 15, double inverted commas added at lines 1, 3 and 5; stanza 21, comma added at line 1; stanza 24, full stop added at line 2; stanza 28, full stop and inverted comma added at line 2; stanza 30, full stop added at lines 2 and 4; stanza 35, inverted commas added at lines 1 and 4; stanza 37, dash added at line 2; stanza 38, full stop added at line 2. See note to 'Ode to a Bowler' (p. 223).

p. 138 'Squat Ursula': f.p. *BN*, pp. 74–6. Source: Bod. Dep. Peake 16, pp. 6^r–6^v. Nonsence 1, p. 10^v, has the title SQUAT URSULA on it, with no poem; hence the conjectural date. Of all Peake's parodies, this is the most obvious, deriving from the hymn 'Jerusalem the Golden' (Bernard of Cluny, trans. J. M. Neale), which begins 'Jerusalem the Golden, / With milk and honey blest'.

p. 140 'The Hideous Root': f.p. *BN*, pp. 59–64, which omits stanzas 13 and 27. Source: Nonsence 1, pp. 4^r–7^v; hence the conjectural date. Stanza 24 was never completed; we have therefore left it in fragmentary form. Punctuation has been changed as follows: a full stop has been added to the end of stanza 9; in stanza 11, a comma has been removed at the end of line 4; in stanza 12, a comma has been removed after 'remembered' at line 1; full stops have been added in stanza 14, line 4, and at the end of stanzas 18 and 20; an exclamation mark has been added at the end of stanza 22; in stanza 23, a full stop has been added at line 2 and Root has been capitalized in line 6; in stanza 27, full stops have been added at lines 2 and 4, a comma at line 5 and an exclamation mark at line 6. Also in stanza 12, the word 'obstructed' has been crossed out and 'confused' inserted in the MS, but we have retained 'obstructed' to preserve the metre (Peake may have intended 'confused *the* deploy of his charms'). See note to 'Ancient Root O Ancient Root' (p. 224).

p. 148 'The Men in Bowler Hats Are Sweet': f.p. *BN*, p. 65. Source: Nonsence 1, p. 36^v; hence the conjectural date. See note to 'Ode to a Bowler' (p. 223).

p. 150 'Aunts and Uncles': f.p. *BN*, pp. 67–71. Source: Peake archive MS. The line 'When Uncle Sid' occurs in Nonsence 1, p. 20^r; the phrase suggests it was the beginning of another poem in the 'Aunts and Uncles' series, and its presence in the 1947 nonsence notebook gives us our conjectural date. See note to 'My Uncle Paul of Pimlico' (p. 226). In her introduction to *BN*, Maeve Gilmore describes the genesis of this series of small poems as follows: 'The short section "Aunts and Uncles" was written in the late 'forties and sprang to some extent from an evening's conversation with friends, when someone who had just returned from a rather remote country holiday mentioned that he had been staying on a farm where there was a gaggle of geese, and that the owner was hardly discernible from his gaggle. The conversation roved upon propinquity, either between a man and a woman, closely related, long married, or any relationship where each partner takes on some of the other's idiosyncrasies – gestures, habits, ideas – so that it is quite difficult to distinguish one from the other. He wrote the rhymes first, and then added the drawings.'

p. 154 'The Osseous 'Orse': f.p. *G*, p. 33, which is our source for all but stanza 4. Stanza 4 was edited out before publication, and is taken from the MS of *G*; we have restored it because it explains why 'The Osseous 'orse sat up at once' in stanza 5. Date given in MS of *G*.

p. 156 'Song of the Castle Poet': unpublished. Source: MS of *G*, which supplies the date.

p. 157 'How White and Scarlet Is that Face': f.p. *G*, p. 309, which is our source. Date given in MS of *G*.

p. 158 'O Here It Is and There It Is…': f.p. *BN*, pp. 46–7. Source: Peake archive MS. Also in Nonsence 2, p. 15^v. A fragment occurs in the MS of *G*, which supplies the date.

p. 161 'Little Spider': f.p. *BN*, p. 22. Source: Bod. Dep Peake 16, p. 7^r. The poem occurs in the MS of *G*, which supplies the date. Versions of the poem are sung by Fuchsia in Peake's adaptation of *TG* for radio (see note to 'Nannie Slagg's Song', p. 231), and by Percy in *WW*. We have based the last four lines of stanza 1 on the *WW* text as the final version.

p. 161 '"It Worries Me to Know"': f.p. *BN*, pp. 23–6. Source: Peake archive MS. Date conjectural, based on the reference to Gormenghast in the final line, which suggests it may have been written while he wrote *G*. It may date from earlier, but the poem's narrative recalls the wooing of Irma Prunesquallor by Bellgrove, so we have opted for the later date. Dashes have been added at stanza 4, line 1 and stanza 15, line 4. In *BN* 'a cloudy-looking man' in line 7 was misread as 'a dowdy-looking man'.

p. 166 'A-Lolling on the Shores of Old Hawaii': f.p. *MP*, p. 72, which is our source; hence the date.

p. 167 'O'er Seas that Have No Beaches': f.p. *MP*, p. 251, which is our source and gives the date. There is another version in Nonsence 2, p. 14. Mr Pye recites these verses as he drinks a farewell glass of wine with his friends. Before the recital he tells them: 'Words at such times make little sense and what sense they do make is nonsense – of which, incidentally, I was once particularly fond. I used to write it once – at board meetings while others doodled. How did that one go…? That particularly good one that I wrote on the back of a procedure form?'

p. 169 'The Bullfrog and the Flies': f.p. *W&D*, p. 96. Source: Peake archive MS, which supplies the date.

p. 170 'The Rhino and the Lark': f.p. *PP*, pp. 499–500, which omits sixteen lines. Source: Peake archive MS, which supplies the date. Inverted comma added at the beginning of line 13.

p. 174 'Richly In the Unctuous Dell': f.p. *PS*, vol. 11, no. 2 (April 2009), p. 13. Source: MS of *MB*, where it is sung by four professors to wake a sleepwalking colleague. Date conjectural.

p. 174 'Manifold Basket's Song': f.p. *PS*, vol. 11, no. 2 (April 2009), p. 13. Source: MS of *MB*. Date conjectural. In the play this 'impromptu little song' is sung by the 'self-absorbed, self-centred' Headmaster of the title.

p. 176 'With a One, Two, Up!': f.p. *PP*, p. 298. Source: MS of *WW*. Date conjectural. Sung by the aged Dr Willy in Act One.

p. 176 'In Ancient Days': f.p. *PP*, p. 354. Source: MS of *WW*. Date conjectural. Sung by the aged Dr Willy in Act Three.

p. 178 'O Keep Away': unpublished. Source: MS of *WW* in the Peake Archive. Date conjectural. This is sung by Sally Devius. According to a note in the archive by Maeve Gilmore, it was written at a time when Peake was thinking of turning *WW* into a musical.

p. 179 'O Darling When a Story's Done': unpublished. Source: MS of *WW* in the Peake archive. Date conjectural. According to a note in the archive by Maeve Gilmore, this song was written at a time when Peake was thinking of turning *WW* into a musical.

p. 181 'Undertaker's Song (1)': unpublished. Source: MS of *WW* in the Peake Archive. Date conjectural. According to a note in the archive by Maeve Gilmore, this song was written at a time when Peake was thinking of turning *WW* into a musical.

p. 182 'Undertaker's Song (2)': unpublished. Source: MS of *WW* in the Peake archive. Date conjectural. According to a note in the archive by Maeve Gilmore, this song was written at a time when Peake was thinking of turning *WW* into a musical.

p. 183 'Nannie Slagg's Song': f.p. *TG: A Radio Play*, *MPR*, no. 21 (1987/8), p. 10. Source: MS in the Peake archive. Date conjectural; the play was broadcast on 1 February 1956. Nannie Slagg sings this to the infant Titus.

p. 183 'Fuchsia's Song': f.p. *TG: A Radio Play*, *MPR*, no. 21 (1987/8), p. 12, which is our source. Date conjectural; the play was broadcast on 1 February 1956.

p. 184 'Nannie Slagg's Lullaby': f.p. *TG: A Radio Play*, *MPR*, no. 21 (1987/8), p. 37, which is our source. Date conjectural; the play was broadcast on 1 February 1956. Nannie Slagg sings this to the infant Titus.

p. 184 'Where the Little Dunderhead': f.p. *TG: A Radio Play*, *MPR*, no. 21 (1987/8), p. 88, which is our source. Date conjectural; the play was broadcast on 1 February 1956. Nannie Slagg sings this to the infant Titus.

p. 186 'Lean Sideways on the Wind': f.p. *BN*, p. 49. Source: Nonsense 2, p. 1^r; hence the conjectural date. See note to 'My Uncle Paul of Pimlico' (p.226).

p. 186 'Of Pygmies, Palms and Pirates': f.p. *BN*, p. 29. Source: Nonsense 2, p. 2^r; hence the conjectural date.

p. 188 'An Angry Cactus Does No Good': f.p. *BN*, p. 37. Source: Nonsense 2, p. 3^r; hence the conjectural date.

p. 189 'I Cannot Give the Reasons': f.p. *BN*, p. 39. Source: Nonsense 2, p. 3^v; hence the conjectural date.

p. 191 'O Little Fly': f.p. *BN*, p. 22. Source: Nonsense 2, p. 4^r; hence the conjectural date.

p. 191 'How Fly the Birds of Heaven': f.p. *TA*, second edition, p. 187, which is our source, except for the last line, which comes from Nonsense 2, p. 5^r. The poem's presence in Nonsense 2 gives the conjectural date. In *TA* the poem is recited by Crabcalf (who describes it as 'a passing thought'), and the last line is commuted into dialogue: 'Crabcalf opened his eyes. "Do you see what I mean?" he said'.

p. 193 'Leave the Stronger': f.p. *BN*, p. 77, where it was accidentally fused with 'Fish or Fowl' (below) as if they were one poem. Source: Nonsense 2, p. 6^r; hence the conjectural date.

p. 194 'Fish or Fowl': f.p. *BN*, p. 77, where it accidentally continues 'Leave the Stronger' (above), and line 5 is missing. Source: Nonsense 2, p. 7^r; hence the conjectural date.

p. 195   '"Shrink! Shrink!"': f.p. *BN*, p. 66. Source: Nonsence 2, p. 8^r; hence the conjectural date.

p. 196   'An Old and Crumbling Parapet': f.p. *BN*, p. 30, where stanzas 1 and 2 are accidentally combined. Source: Nonsence 2, p. 9^r; hence the conjectural date.

p. 198   'It Is Most Best': f.p. *BN*, p. 31. Source: Nonsence 2, p. 10^r; hence the conjectural date.

p. 198   'The Hours of Night Are Drawing On': unpublished. Source: Nonsence 2, p. 10^v; hence the conjectural date.

p. 200   'Over the Pig-Shaped Clouds They Flew': unpublished. Source: Nonsence 2, p. 11^r; hence the conjectural date.

p. 200   'Come, Break the News to Me, Sweet Horse!': f.p. *BN*, p. 35, where 'kissed' in stanza 4 is given as 'kicked'. Source: Nonsence 2, pp. 12^r and 14^v; hence the conjectural date.

p. 202   'What Though My Jaw': unpublished. Source: Nonsence 2, p. 12^v; hence the conjectural date.

p. 202   'The Trouble with Geraniums': f.p. *BN*, p. 41, where 'crows' in line 9 is given as 'stars'. Source: Nonsence 2, p. 13^r; hence the conjectural date.

p. 203   'Crocodiles': f.p. *BN*, p. 43. Source: Nonsence 2, p. 15^r; hence the conjectural date.

p. 204   'Along the Cold, Regurgitating Shore': f.p. *BN*, p. 45, where it is accidentally printed as part of 'O Love, O Death, O Ecstasy' (p. 127). Source: Nonsence 2, p. 16^v; hence the conjectural date. The original reads 'regurting' for 'regurgitating', but rhyme and sense suggest that this is a slip on Peake's part.

p. 204   'I Have My Price': f.p. *TA*, pp. 54–5, where it is described as 'a sort of song' sung to Juno by Muzzlehatch. This is our source. Another version occurs in Nonsence 2, p. 16^v; hence the conjectural date. In this version lines 7 and 8 read: 'From yellow grass in Paraguay / Where knitting is taboo', and lines 13–15 read 'O felony in Paraguay, / There's not a soul in Paraguay / Who's worth the dreaming of'. In addition, the word 'pearl' in line 9 is spelt 'purl'.

p. 205   'Jehovah, Jehovah': f.p. Act III of *The Cave* in *MPR*, no. 29 (1996) [no pagination], which reproduces a TS of Peake's play that was circulated by his agent c. 1960. From this the play can be dated to the late 1950s.

pp. 208, **211**   'Over the Border, or The Adventures of Footfruit'; 'The Adventures of Footfruit, or The Enthusiast': f.p. *BN*, pp. 79–87. Source: Peake archive TS. Date conjectural. Maeve Gilmore writes about the story as follows in the introduction to *BN*: '"The Adventures of Footfruit", which is the last piece in this book, is also the last he conceived. It was to have been a short book. Its genesis was an article in the *News Chronicle* of 25 September 1957, headed:

SUB-THINK
sub-Think
Sub-Think

"They're going to try it on us soon," the article began, continuing: "A company was recently formed in the United States with the blatant aim of taking hold of the human mind, without the owner's consent, much less his co-operation. The company is called the Subliminal Projection Corporation."'

p. 217 'Another Draft of Footfruit': f.p. *New Worlds*, no. 187 (February 1969), pp. 41–3, which is our source, having been reproduced in facsimile from an MS of which we have traced only one page. Date conjectural (above, note to 'Over the Border, or The Adventures of Footfruit'). Comma added in the phrase 'What, no reply?'. The name of the dog here, 'Jackpot', recalls the name of the Lost Uncle's companion, Jackson, in Peake's illustrated novel *Letters from a Lost Uncle* (1948). It also suggests that the dog has won what the narrator desires, proximity to Footfruit (whose name in conjunction with the dog's evokes a fruit machine or one-armed bandit).

p. 220 'Crown Me With Hairpins': f.p. *BN*, p. 73. Source: Bod. Dep. Peake 16, p. 16^v. Date unknown.

Key to the Figures of Speech

Light fingered	20
Keeping his end up	25
Scraping an acquaintance	28
Paddle your own canoe!	32
A bird in the hand is worth two in the bush	33
Getting his sea-legs	46
I could kick myself	51
It suits them down to the ground	52
Splitting hairs	57
Keeping his chin up	62
Getting his back up	66
Cold comfort	67
Getting down to brass tacks	70
Put that in your pipe and smoke it	74
I have other fish to fry	118
His right-hand man	129
Cooling his heels	145
Horse-play	155
Sitting pretty	163
Love me, love my dog!	168
Led by the nose	171
To cut a long story short	185
Toeing the line	190
It came to a head	192
Burning their bridges	197
Grin and bear it	199
Bringing him down to earth	206
Coming up to scratch	207
Severing relations	219

Index of Titles

About My Ebb and Flow-ziness — 42
The Adventures of Footfruit or The Enthusiast — 211
Again! Again! and Yet Again — 112
All Over the Lilac Brine! — 78
A-Lolling on the Shores of Old Hawaii — 166
Along the Cold, Regurgitating Shore — 204
Although I Love Him — 26
An Angry Cactus Does No Good — 188
An Old and Crumbling Parapet — 196
Ancient Root O Ancient Root — 44
Another Draft of Footfruit: Chapter 1 — 217
Aunts and Uncles — 150

The Ballad of Sweet Pighead — 116
Beard of My Chin — 26
The Bullfrog and the Flies — 169

The Camel — 96
Come, Break the News to Me, Sweet Horse! — 200
Come Husband! Come, and Ply the Trade — 69
Come, Sit Beside Me Dear, He Said — 60
The Crocodile — 82
Crocodiles — 203
Crown Me with Hairpins — 220

Deliria — 63
The Dwarf of Battersea — 35

A Fair Amount of Doziness — 43
Fish or Fowl — 194
The Frivolous Cake — 44
Fuchsia's Song — 183

The Giraffe	84
Green Park	24
The Hideous Root	140
The Hippopotamus	102
The Hours of Night Are Drawing On	198
Hold Fast	120
How Fly the Birds of Heaven	191
How Good It Is to Be Alone (1)	71
How Good It Is to Be Alone (2)	73
How Mournful to Imagine	92
How White and Scarlet Is that Face	157
I Cannot Give the Reasons	189
I Cannot Give You Reasons	115
I Cannot Simply Stand and Watch	58
I Have My Price	204
I Married Her in Green	50
I Must Begin to Comprehend	122
I Saw a Puffin	21
I Waxes and I Wanes, Sir	100
I Wish I Could Remember	98
In Ancient Days	176
It Is Most Best	198
It Makes a Change	88
'It Worries Me to Know'	161
The Jailor and the Jaguar	94
Jehovah, Jehovah	205
The King of Ranga-Tanga-Roon	114
A Languorous Life	104
Lean Sideways on the Wind	186
Leave the Stronger	193
Linger Now with Me, Thou Beauty	48
Little Spider	161
Manifold Basket's Song	174
The Men in Bowler Hats Are Sweet	148
Mine Was the One	65
My Uncle Paul of Pimlico	86

Nannie Slagg's Lullaby	184
Nannie Slagg's Song	183
Norbury	23
O Darling When a Story's Done	179
O Here It Is and There It Is…	158
O Keep Away	178
O Little Fly	191
O Love, O Death, O Ecstasy	127
Ode to a Bowler	30
O'er Seas that Have No Beaches	167
Of Pygmies, Palms and Pirates	186
One Day When They Had Settled Down	110
The Osseous 'Orse	154
Over the Pig-Shaped Clouds They Flew	200
Practically Poetry	29
Raft Song of the Conger Eel	31
Railway Ditties	23
The Rhino and the Lark	170
Richly in the Unctuous Dell	174
Roll Them Down	108
Sensitive, Seldom and Sad	106
'Shrink! Shrink!'	195
Simple, Seldom and Sad	47
Song of the Castle Poet	156
The Song of Lien Tsung	22
Squat Ursula	138
Streatham and Balham	23
The Sunlight Lies Upon the Fields	64
The Sunlight Falls Upon the Grass	80
Swelter's Song	53
Synopsis: Over the Border or The Adventures of Footfruit	208
Thank God for a Tadpole	42
Thornton Heath	23
The Threads of Thought Are Not for Me	68
The Threads Remain	123
Tintinnabulum	128
The Trouble with Geraniums	202

Uncle George	113
Undertaker's Song (1)	181
Undertaker's Song (2)	182
Upon My Golden Backbone	76
Upon the Summit of a Hill	59
Waddon	23
What a Day It's Been!	90
What Though My Jaw	202
Where the Little Dunderhead	184
White Mules at Prayer	124
With a One, Two, Up!	176
You Before Me	26
You Can Never Be Sure of Your Birron	24

Index of First Lines

A Crocodile in ecstasy	82
A fair amount of doziness	43
A freckled and frivolous cake there was	44
A languorous life I lead, I do	104
A Plumber appeared by the Light of the Moon	140
About my ebb and flow-ziness	42
Again! again! and yet again	112
All alone	183
A-lolling on the shores of old Hawaii	166
Along my weary whiskers	98
Along the cold, regurgitating	204
Although I love him and could never find	26
Although you may not understand it	22
An angry cactus does no good	188
An old and crumbling parapet	196
Ancient Root O Ancient Root	44
Around the shores of the Arrogant Isles	78
Beard of my chin, white product of my jaw	26
'Come, break the news to me, Sweet Horse	200
Come, flick the ulna juggler-wise	154
'Come, sit beside me dear,' he said	60
Crown me with hairpins intertwined	220
Dear children, what a day it's been!	90
Deliria was seven foot five	110
Fish or fowl, it's all the same	194
Footfruit, a healthy, happy man, crosses the border	208
Give me food 'n' drink 'n' fun	53

He must be an artist…	29
Hold fast	120
How fly the birds of heaven save by their wings?	191
How good it is to be alone (1)	71
How good it is to be alone (2)	73
How otherwise can I unfold myself	217
How white and scarlet is that face!	157
I always cast a Mental Wreath	23
I cannot give the Reasons	189
I cannot give you reasons	115
I cannot simply stand and watch	58
I have my price: it's rather high	204
I married her in green	50
I must begin to comprehend	122
I saw a camel sit astride	96
I saw a Puffin	21
I watched a camel sit astride	63
I waxes, and I wanes, sir	100
In ancient days, oh in ancient days	176
It is most best	198
'It worries me to know,' she cried	161
Jehovah, Jehovah	205
Lean sideways on the wind, and if it bears	186
Leave the stronger	193
Linger now with me, thou Beauty	48
Little spider	161
Look!	211
Mine was the One. Mine was the two	65
My Uncle Paul of Pimlico	86
Never look eager, friends	182
Never mind	183
O here it is! and there it is!	158
O keep away	178
O little fly! delightful fly!	191
O love, O death, O ecstasy	127
O'er seas that have no beaches	167

Of pygmies, palms and pirates	186
Oh, Hat that cows the spirit!	30
Oh why is Streatham Common	23
Once upon a time there was a Rhino	170
Once upon the Banks of a Green Stream	169
Our Ears, you know, have Other Uses	92
Over the pig-shaped clouds they flew	200
Pretty heart be quiet, then	184
Richly in the Unctuous Dell	174
Roll them down	108
Sally: O darling when a story's done	179
Sensitive, Seldom and Sad are we	106
She.	69
She stared at him as hard as she	203
'Shrink! Shrink!' said I	195
Simple, seldom and sad	47
Snobbery S'Norbury	23
So is it always when the hairfaced hedgerow	156
Squat Ursula the golden	138
Strangul'm, scragle'm	31
Sweet Pighead, youngest of the family	116
Thank God for a tadpole!	42
The hours of night are drawing on	198
The Jailor and the Jaguar	94
The King of Ranga-Tanga-Roon	114
The Men in Bowler Hats are Sweet!	148
The sunlight falls upon the grass	80
The sunlight lies upon the fields	64
The threads of thought are not for me	68
The threads remain, and cotton ones	123
The trouble with geraniums	202
The very nastiest grimace	102
There lived a dwarf in Battersea	37
There was a man came up to me	128
There's nothing makes a Greenland Whale	88
Tiddle-ti-pompa	174
To our primordial calling	181

Uncle George became so nosey	113
Upon my golden backbone	76
Upon the summit of a hill	59
Whad'n earth would I do if I lived in Waddon?	23
What could be greener	24
What though my jaw be long and blue	202
When Aunty Jane	150
Where the little dunderhead	184
White mules at prayer! Ignore them. Turn to me	124
With a one, two, up!	176
Ye olde Ballade concerning ye yellow dwarfe of Battersea	35
You before me	26
You can never be sure of your Birron	24
You may think that he's rather slow	84